The Poetry
of Capital

The Poetry
of Capital

Voices from Twenty-First-Century America

Edited by
Benjamin S. Grossberg and Clare Rossini

THE UNIVERSITY OF WISCONSIN PRESS

Publication of this book has been made possible, in part, through support from the Brittingham Trust.

The University of Wisconsin Press
728 State Street, Suite 443
Madison, Wisconsin 53706
uwpress.wisc.edu

Gray's Inn House, 127 Clerkenwell Road
London ECIR 5DB, United Kingdom
eurospanbookstore.com

Printed in the United States of America
This book may be available in a digital edition.

Library of Congress Cataloging-in-Publication Data
Names: Grossberg, Benjamin S. (Benjamin Scott), 1971– editor. |
    Rossini, Clare, editor.
Title: The poetry of capital : voices from twenty-first-century America / edited by
    Benjamin S. Grossberg and Clare Rossini.
Description: Madison, Wisconsin : The University of Wisconsin Press, [2020]
Identifiers: LCCN 2020017804 | ISBN 9780299330446 (paperback)
Subjects: LCSH: Money—United States—Poetry. |
    Wealth—United States—Poetry. | American poetry—21st century. |
    United States—Economic conditions—Poetry. | LCGFT: Poetry.
Classification: LCC PS595.M59 P64 2020 | DDC 811/.60803553—dc23
LC record available at https://lccn.loc.gov/2020017804

Contents

From the Editors   xi

ALAN CHAZARO   3
   El Paletero's Song   4
   The Cowboy Shirts   5

ARICKA FOREMAN   8
   Still Life of Acme in Spring   9
   Price of Today's Ticket   10
   Before I Fire Her, the Therapist Asks *What IS It Like to*
     Be a Black Woman HERE: A Monologue   10
   October   11

CLAIRE MCQUERRY   14
   Textbook Ekphrasis   15

WILL CORDEIRO   20
   Piecework   21
   Smoke   22
   Spambot   23

ROSS WHITE   26
   Savings & Loan   27
   Dark Money   28

DIANA MARIE DELGADO   30
   Free Cheese and Butter   31
   Man of the House   31
   La Puente   32

XOCHIQUETZAL CANDELARIA   34
  Surrender #4: Take Notice, Take Nothing   35
  Matter   36
  Boom   37

ROBERT AVERY   39
  The Leisure Class   40
  Odds Are   41

CRYSTAL WILLIAMS   43
  Detroit as Brewster Projects   44
  At the Water   46

CATE MARVIN   50
  Stopping for Gas Near Cheat Lake   51
  Stone Fruit   51

KEVIN PRUFER   55
  The Vast Economies   56
  True Crime   57

MAJOR JACKSON   59
  Selling Out   60
  A Brief Reflection on Torture Near the Library of Congress   62

SUSAN BRIANTE   64
  from Mother Is Marxist   65

SHERYL LUNA   69
  Not One Red Cent   70
  Chico's Tacos   70
  The Loser   72

ERIC GANSWORTH   75
  A Half-Life of Cardio-Pulmonary Function   76
  Wade Wakes Me with Sweat, Tears, and, Yes, the Rest Too   78

DEVON BALWIT   81
  Un-American   82
  Minding the Gap   82
  invocation   83

DENISE DUHAMEL 85
  $100,000 86
  $400,000 87
  $600,000 88

KATHLEEN WINTER 90
  Country Club Fourth of July 91
  The Grammar of Ornament 91
  Hipster Squid 92

JANE MEAD 94
  Money 95
  from Cove 95

ALLISON HEDGE COKE 99
  Off-Season 100
  This He Learned by Being American 101
  Wealth 102

JAMES FOWLER 106
  The School for Lucre 107

MARTÍN ESPADA 111
  Who Burns for the Perfection of Paper 112
  The Saint Vincent de Paul Food Pantry Stomp 112
  Offerings to an Ulcerated God 113

JO PITKIN 116
  Village: Closure 117
  Village: Food Chain 117
  Village: Can Collector 117
  Village: White Money 118

KIMIKO HAHN 120
  Things That Remind Me of Squalor 121
  Constant Objection 121

DAVID BAKER 124
  Midwest: Ode 125
  Postmodernism 126

JOSEPH GASTIGER   129
  The Industrial Age   130
  Parable of Untraceable Power   130
  Hamelin   131

TONY HOAGLAND   133
  America   134
  Big Grab   135

DAVID WOJAHN   138
  Ghost Mall: Richmond, Virginia   139
  Piñata   140

MARK DOTY   144
  Air Rights   145

JANE HIRSHFIELD   152
  In My Wallet I Carry a Card   153
  My Luck   153
  Three-Legged Blues   154

DORIANNE LAUX   156
  Waitress   157
  The Tooth Fairy   158

AFAA MICHAEL WEAVER   161
  Ivory Soap, a Whiteness   162
  A Postscript to Giant   163
  Repack Room   164

KATHLEEN HELLEN   166
  The Dirty Work of Quarters   167
  How Light Bends at the Exxon   167
  The Erotic Has No Use   168

DANA GIOIA   170
  Money   171
  Shopping   171

JOHN BRADLEY   174
  What Money Can Buy   175
  As Blood Is the Fruit of the Heart   176

EDWARD HIRSCH   179
  Mergers and Acquisitions   180
  Cold Calls   180
  Liberty Brass   181
  Second-Story Warehouse   182

YUSEF KOMUNYAKAA   185
  A Prayer for Workers   186
  Cape Coast Castle   187

MARY JO BANG   190
  A Woman Overheard Speaking   191
  Wall Street   191

MINNIE BRUCE PRATT   193
  Looking for Work   194
  Picketing the Bargain Store   194
  Playing the Guitar Underground   195
  The Dow Turns Red   196

GEORGE PERREAULT   198
  Buster McKinney: Economics   199
  James Hardesty: Burrito   200

SHARON OLDS   202
  Left-Wife Bop   203
  Money   204

WENDY BARKER   206
  Planishing   207
  Tombstone, 1962   207
  On Silver Spoons   207
  Cleaning Silver   208

ROBERT PINSKY   210
  Shirt   211
  The Refinery   212

MARTHA COLLINS   215
  Middle   216
  White Money   218

For Further Reading   221
Acknowledgments   223

From the Editors

This anthology began with a concern and a core belief. First, the concern. Wealth in the United States has been concentrating into fewer and fewer hands for decades, a phenomenon that the COVID-19 pandemic has made painfully visible (more on this later). In 2011, in the aftermath of the Occupy Wall Street movement, people began talking about "the 1 percent": the notion that a tiny group of Americans control much of the wealth in our country. It didn't take much digging for us to realize that this cohort is actually much smaller than 1 percent. In fact, the top *tenth* of 1 percent of American citizens control more wealth than the entire bottom 90 percent. Fifty million of us—more than one-seventh of the entire population—live in poverty, while two hundred families each have a net worth of more than a billion dollars. We mulled that statistic. What is the human cost of such disparity? Is the trend of wealth concentration reversible—and if not, what are the long-term implications for the future of our country?

And then the core belief. We believe that poetry lays bare human stakes in a way nothing else can, often with a vivid immediacy which manages at the same time to be nonreductive: to make us *feel*, and to make us feel *the whole truth*, even if we can't trace exactly the mechanism by which that truth has been communicated. We believe that if you really want to understand the shape of something, its complexity and its textures, go see what the poets have to say.

So that's what we did. We consulted poets. We put out a call for poems for this anthology, asking for work about income inequality, yes, but also about all the ways capital shapes our lives and those of our fellow citizens. We made the call as broad as possible because we wanted to learn—not to proscribe but to be educated.

From the start, we understood that this collection would be political. As we considered wealth distribution, we came to see our moment as a pivot point, a juncture when the increasing polarization of wealth is stressing our country in a way that could prove unsustainable. It was our sense when we started, and years of reading for this anthology has only confirmed the impression, that this increasing inequity is not compatible with the foundations of democracy, such as the decentralization of power and mutuality between the governors and the governed. And we see increasing wealth inequity as a political problem, meaning that the ways to best address it would be enacted by a political process.

But we hoped that this anthology would be a sociological project, too, because poems about money reveal who we are with a clarity no data can conjure. In contemporary America, money reaches deep, structuring our relations with each other in the way age or social caste does in other societies. And we understood that this anthology would have a psychological dimension, too, because we imagined that poems about money would really be poems about how our minds work: how we value ourselves, how we understand our place in the world.

That said, we did not want this to be an *ideological* anthology, pushing a particular policy agenda. Can an anthology be political but not ideological? Frankly, we're not sure. Maybe the best we can hope for is a soft-focus filter on our ideological stance. But we can say this: we resisted poems whose sole raison d'être was a policy agenda. We wanted always human stakes.

To that end, we chose to limit the number of contributors to this anthology to forty-four poets. By including fewer poets but using a larger selection of work by each, we hope to come closer to representing whole viewpoints—individuals, socially and culturally embedded, writing out of their lives. We want readers to get a sense of larger projects. We believe that this is an especially humanistic strategy, moving toward a fuller presentation of who we are as Americans.

In addition, we asked these forty-four poets to step out from behind their work in short prose statements, in which they might ruminate on the subject of money and poetry in any way they saw fit. We tried to be as open as possible in our parameters for these statements, letting the poets follow their own concerns. Some dilated on the life experiences behind their poems, adding detail and meditating more fully than the lyric form might allow. Others reached further back, evoking formative experiences with capital, informing their poems in oblique ways. And still others glanced at wider cultural contexts or considered the work of poetry more broadly. As these prose statements are the work of poets, some are rich with music and imagery and feel almost like unlineated poems. This variety of approaches—essayistic, biographical, and lyrical—is just what we hoped for: fresh contexts, new ways into the work, and deeper engagement with whole people.

But who to include in the book? The project might have begun with the seventeenth century. From James Revel, Phillis Wheatley, and the Lowell Mill Girls; to Fanny Fern and Walt Whitman; to Langston Hughes, Muriel Rukeyser, Gwendolyn Brooks, and Philip Levine, the poetry of capital has always been a critical current in American literary culture. But we believe that the urgent conversation our country is having about income inequality and wealth distribution calls for contemporary witnesses, poets writing about the ways our economic system is currently empowering or failing us, and our democracy. So we chose to focus this anthology on people writing now, in twenty-first-century America.

Given that our approach restricted the number of poets we could include, we were attracted to the model of an anthology based on the principle of demographic sampling. On first blush, one might imagine such an anthology containing as close a representation of American diversity as possible, with each poet speaking in a first-person voice, reflecting his or her first-hand experience. And a diversity of contributors was a prime consideration as we chose poets—diversity of race, class, gender, and sexual orientation. We also grew aware that some experiences explored in the poems seemed linked to the age of the poet. To underscore those continuities, we ordered the anthology by generation, beginning with the youngest contributors.

But the dangers of an anthology built solely on a demographic approach seemed clear, as well. It sells American poetry short by suggesting a limited model of what a poem can do. Poetry is not always a record of a poet's individual experience; it can be an act of imagination or of empathy. That is, poetry can look outward, beyond the self, rather than inward. We saw, also, the danger of suggesting that poets are representatives of their ethnographic or subcultural groups. So, while we understood the power of the first-person voice and the necessity of demographic diversity, we felt compelled to avoid any suggestion of poet-as-spokesperson and to include a variety of poetic approaches.

We were especially interested, then, in including poems written in third-person. For example, Jo Pitkin's poems survey a range of villagers, many of whom, unlike the poet, made out just fine in the Great Recession of 2008. Kevin Prufer's "The Vast Economies," with its mythic sensibility, suggests disturbing human analogues as he portrays animals—leopards, hyenas, gazelles—musing on the necessity of currency as they go about the business of predator, scavenger, and prey. Such third-person approaches speak to the work of the American poet, to "sing America"—Whitman's phrase—and catalogue our great diversity, including those who have, whether by necessity or predisposition, taken up other work in the world. We especially understood that the dramatic monologue might be risky in an anthology like ours, since the form, even as it presents other lives, potentially displaces those who live those lives. But we also felt that, at its best, the form enacts empathy, and that it can bring to the table experiences which might otherwise be all but inaccessible. So we have the poems of George Perreault, whose speakers offer life lessons as they might have been passed down in the context of family intimacy, rather than in a more removed voice.

So what will readers discover in *The Poetry of Capital?* Below we discuss some of the major themes and issues found in these poems.

History, Economic Forces, and Global Capitalism

Many of the poets in this anthology address the shared big-picture economic shocks of the last hundred years. These poems serve to remind us that our moment has causes and precedents, that it is historically embedded. And they further demonstrate that our attitudes and understandings, too, are historically embedded.

Two of the poets here contextualize their current relationship with capital by reaching back to what their family members experienced in the 1930s, another time of world economic crisis. Claire McQuerry's "Textbook Ekphrasis" documents how the Great Depression lives on in her grandmother, who describes the brutal realities of chronic unemployment and breadlines. Even in old age, the grandmother packs extra food into her purse from a restaurant buffet, explaining "You never know . . . where your next lunch is gonna come from, Sugar." This recollection provides context for the Great Depression's namesake, the Great Recession of 2008. Writing in the midst of that financial downturn, McQuerry herself faces similar challenges, scraping together fifty cents to purchase a flower pot at a yard sale for a neighbor struggling to pay her bills. Paralleling McQuerry's poem, Allison Hedge Coke's "Wealth" recalls the Dustbowl of the 1930s, the series

of droughts that decimated U.S. agricultural production and suffocated live-
stock, destroying the health and livelihood of Americans across the Great
Plains. Native Americans in the Midwest, already impoverished, were par-
ticularly hard hit. "Wealth" documents the generosity of the poet's Chero-
kee grandparents during these hard times, reflecting an ethic of giving that
shapes future generations. When the poor come wanting, Hedge Coke says,
"We pull out our checkbooks, cards, / overdraw ourselves. / Feed them."

Ross White also reaches back, tackling the savings and loan crisis of
the 1980s and 1990s, which permanently shuttered more than a thousand
banks nationwide. White's melancholy "Savings and Loan" parallels famil-
ial and national economic dysfunction. The poet's parents are divorcing,
and federal banking regulators come knocking at the door of the fam-
ily home. Yet, strikingly, this poem is not simply about past crises. White
begins sentence after sentence with the verb "Occupy." This passionate use
of anaphora insists on the context for his reminiscence, the Occupy Wall
Street movement, which began in 2011 and became a national grassroots
drive to resist economic inequity.

Other poems focus solely on contemporary, big-picture economic trends.
But these trends, too, are distilled in the human stakes that poetry is par-
ticularly well suited to explore. Joseph Gastiger's "Parable of Untraceable
Power" takes on "dark money," those vast sums of cash funneled by wealthy
individuals, corporations, and other organizations through nonprofits, used
to bankroll political causes and campaigns. Legalized by the Supreme Court's
Citizens United decision of 2010, these hidden donations have radically
changed American political life. Gastiger characterizes dark money as a
pernicious virus infecting technology, the banking system, tax codes—even
nature and our bodies. Another disturbing economic trend is dissected in
Tony Hoagland's "Big Grab," a darkly comic exposé of corporate marketing
practices. The management in Hoagland's fictional corn chip company
decides to raise profits by cutting back on the amount of chips included in
individual bags. As Hoagland wryly notes, "So the concept of Big is quietly
modified / to mean *More or Less Large, or Only Slightly Less Big than Before.*"
The poet connects such bottom-line tactics to the debasement of language:
words "get crookeder and crookeder."

In recent decades, the global nature of capitalism has been accelerated by
new technologies, the growth of multinational corporations, and relaxed
regulations on trade. As a result, most of the products we consume acquire

a complex provenance in their journey to our shopping bags, raising vexing moral questions. In "Shirt," Robert Pinsky exposes the pan-continental network of agriculture and industry that supports the production of the clothes we wear. David Wojahn's "Piñata" opens in a similar vein in its focus on the ethics of mass production. The poem is set at a holiday gathering of university faculty and staff, at which a piñata of "the President" is a festive prop. Though all proceeds from the party will go to the American Civil Liberties Union, evidencing the revelers' progressive values, the piñata was produced by child laborers who were paid $2.50 a day in a Mexican sweatshop.

Pinsky and Wojahn remind us of the workers in massive factories here and abroad, far removed from the consumers who buy their products. Minnie Bruce Pratt's "Playing the Guitar Underground" provides a detailed portrait of one of those workers. The guitar player's homelessness and poverty are a result of NAFTA, "el tratado de libre comercio," the trade agreement among Mexican, Canada, and the U.S. which was originally signed into law in 1993. The terms of that trade agreement allowed U.S. agribusiness to flood the Mexican market with subsidized corn, making it nearly impossible for rural Mexican families—already living in dire poverty—to support themselves through their small-scale farming practices.

Pratt's poem reminds us that, as a nation created by people who came to this land from other nations and continents, we are steeped in the cultural, political, and economic realities of immigration. A number of poets in our collection explore that reality, focusing especially on the commercial and cultural exchange across our southern border. Alan Chazaro's "The Cowboy Shirts" introduces us to Fortunato, who is "secreted North" to begin a new life. In America, Fortunato makes a living doing hard manual labor with the "cash-only" payments accorded illegal immigrants. Frustrated with his drinking and gambling, his family threatens to call immigration officials. But they hesitate: "how could we— / the children of immigrants / ourselves?" And Sheryl Luna takes us on a granular tour of "Chico's Tacos," a restaurant in the southern border town of El Paso, where "twin barbed wire / stretches across the river to protect freedom." As Luna notes, "It's really cash" being protected, "and everyone feels it." Yet here, too, people find a way to live. For all the economic hardship of the area—factories closed, west Texas oil men going bust—people return to Chico's. "It's something of home, / something to be found nowhere else."

The down-home atmosphere of Chico's Tacos reminds us that, despite globalism, a variety of local businesses and economies continue to thrive.

David Baker writes about one such business, an Amish market in Ohio, whose intimacy he pointedly contrasts with "the corporate farm five miles away." Baker emphasizes the human dimension of this market: "There are field things hand-wrought of applewood / and oak, and oiled at the palm of one man." And in "Waitress," Dorianne Laux reviews the grueling hours put in for a restaurant job. Her prose statement, however, suggests that the job had another dimension, one familiar to many in the working world. When any among them was in financial difficulty, Laux tells us, her fellow waitresses "chipped in to help" with rent, food, doctors' bills, birthday gifts. Laux's description points toward the phenomenon of "the gift economy," a system of exchange in which valuables are freely given, with no expectation that anything will be given in return. As Laux puts it, "No one ever wanted for anything in a family of waitresses."

Labor

How do we first come to know money? Perhaps as physical objects—something to see, touch, feel, like the proverbial lucky penny in Hirshfield's "My Luck," lying there in the road. Coins and bills may be singular in this regard: What other items pass through the hands of all of us? But for many, it is our first experiences with work that move money beyond object or novelty into a shaping force, alternately vexing and empowering as we come to understand that we, too, must—suggestive phrase!—"make a living." Many of our poets write about this early experience with work. In "What Money Can Buy," John Bradley describes the pleasure of purchasing comic books and candy with quarters earned on the paper route he had as a boy. But Bradley's college job thrusts him into a quandary: he unwittingly becomes an accomplice to a landlord who is evicting cash-strapped tenants. The fourteen-year-old speaker in Will Cordeiro's "Piecework" has a similar epiphany regarding the moral complexity often involved in making money. As he plies the backbreaking labor of harvesting crops on a large farm, he comes to see that for his fellows—migrant laborers and "old poor blacks"— the job is a livelihood, while for him it's "only a crummy summer job." Major Jackson's "Selling Out" also documents a formative work experience, as payment for a double shift at McDonald's leaves a pair of friends feeling flush with "the power of our riches." But the friends' neighborhood is gritty and ultimately dangerous; the young men get tangled in a drug deal that leaves the speaker with a "square barrel prodding a temple." In Jackson's experience, corporate America—here manifested in a fast-food franchise—

comes up against the shadow world of drug dealing: two economic forces that shape and rend so many American communities.

Many of our poets explore the world of adult work—some with humor. Denise Duhamel's "$400,000" provides a taxonomy of the job spectrum, from blue-collar to professional-managerial class. The poet's uncle, "a big mucky-muck in a supermarket chain," gives the poet a cashier job at one of his stores, and the poet's friends, who work in gas stations and factories, label her job "cushy" for its annual raises and overtime pay. Later, Duhamel's rich uncle meets Frank Perdue, the chicken magnate, and, in their stinginess, the two haggle over who will pay the odd cent of a shared coffee-shop bill. That air of comic absurdity also saturates James Fowler's "School for Lucre," which caricatures the managerial class through the lens of a fictional business school. The school boasts a "campus Lothario" who "woos unsuspecting / pension funds," and features "financial engineers" who invent "the nillo," a financial instrument "seven times removed / from any actual commodity." Mary Jo Bang, too, employs wit—though of a darker cast—in her poem "Wall Street," with its half-chilling, half-humorous refrain. Bang renders the voice of a banker speaking to "Monsignor," both insulated in their privilege. "I'm certain God wishes me well," the banker confides, betraying an astonishing degree of entitlement as he justifies his success in moral terms.

In contrast to Bang's focus on the wealthy, Afaa Michael Weaver looks at the other end of the economic spectrum. He focuses directly on the physical, mental, and emotional toll often exacted by labor. In "Ivory Soap, a Whiteness," Weaver, who worked for years in the Baltimore factories of Bethlehem Steel and Proctor and Gamble, observes that, in the factory, "masters . . . sit in invisible places," then speaks of "the holds of ships filthy" and "a nation / obese with forgetting." Weaver is asking us to consider whether these workers are that far removed from the Africans brought here in ships to toil in the fields and households of American masters.

Finally, Diana Marie Delgado points us toward the labor we may do when conventional opportunities to earn money are unavailable to us or insufficient to our needs. In "Man of the House," the poet's brother returns home after having stolen a purse, and their father snaps: "Who does he think he is / bringing home finery?" The father's objection—unexpected and ironic—isn't on moral grounds but is rather an accusation of pretense. Delgado notes in her statement that she saw "a strong competition emerge, as if my brother was outshining my dad." At issue here is who is bringing home sufficient means, not how those means are earned. The poet reminds us that moral judgments often fail to hold up in the face of economic necessity.

Social Equity

How do race, class, and gender structure the experience of capital? Some of the poets here reach out to broader contexts, including historical and international narratives, reminding us that the distribution of wealth in America is not random or accidental but the result of long-standing power inequities. Other poets look inward to their personal experience of race, class, or gender to consider how their relative economic empowerment may be tied to these identities. Taken together, the poets suggest complex inter-sectionalities, exploring how most of us are both exploited and bolstered by the flow of capital.

On the question of race, Yusef Komunyakaa and Martha Collins take a big-picture approach. These poets investigate one of the fundamental shaping forces of the contemporary American economy, its evolution from a system of slavery. In "Cape Coast Castle," Komunyakaa returns to the roots of the slave trade in a global economy. The poet tours one of the many Guyanese castles built and inhabited by European colonizers, their dungeons the last stop for African people being shipped to American plantations. The castle's forbidding architecture and the violence that occurred within—including the rape and beating at the poem's end—haunt the poet as he continues his travels. Collins's "White Money" approaches the inter-section of race and capital from a different angle, using collage. In stripped-down language, the poet asks us to consider the relationship among three phenomena: the engravings of slaves found on antebellum Southern currency; the payments made in 1956 by *Look* magazine to the murderers of Emmet Till, in exchange for the rights to publish their story of his murder; and, finally, a seemingly innocuous marketing message from a contemporary intellectual property rights company, Whitemoney.com. Collins's examples point to how money, racism, and violence have been inextricably intertwined throughout American history, a reality that social media has made impossible to avoid, most recently in the 2020 killings of Ahmaud Arbery, Breonna Taylor, and George Floyd.

Martín Espada's "Offerings to an Ulcerated God" dramatizes the less visible but equally destructive racism in a legal system that historically has failed the poor and persons of color. A woman seeks financial redress against a landlord who refuses to perform basic maintenance, but she is denied her day in court because she doesn't speak English: "The judge called for an interpreter, / but all the interpreters were gone." Aricka Foreman's "Before I Fire Her, the Therapist Asks *What IS It Like to Be a Black Woman HERE*: A Monologue" is also deeply concerned with the enmeshment of language and racism. The poem provides cringeworthy examples of microaggressions often faced by persons of color, and the white commentators' references to Detroit betray their superficial understanding of race and economic hardship.

And in "Things That Remind Me of Squalor," Kimiko Hahn investigates the experience of race and capital beyond a white/nonwhite binary. Writing in a list form inspired by the tenth-century Japanese poet Sei Shonagon, Hahn mulls an eBay find, a "little black boy" doll that is *"holding watermelon and sitting on potty."* Produced in occupied Japan and marketed to American soldiers, the object was designed to appeal to racially loaded sensibilities. Hahn, herself of Asian descent, confesses that she already has two such dolls. She finds them "charming" and asks: Does purchasing something with a "racist aspect . . . make me a racist?" The question hangs at the end of a stanza, inviting readers to consider their own complicity.

The poems exploring the connection between gender and capital are often intimate, employing first-person accounts of how money shapes workplace, romantic, and familial relationships. A number of these poems take on sexual harassment. In others, capital informs dynamics of love and alienation, as filtered through traditional gender roles. What are the implications of a woman receiving a gift from a man or a son watching his father sweat over money?

Cate Marvin's "Stone Fruit" juxtaposes traditional female roles vis-à-vis men—support staff and homemaker—revealing both as a betrayal. The poet is an amanuensis, earning money by furthering the work of "an important man" who sexually harasses her. She is also a romantic partner, trying to save enough to be a homemaker; the poet wants to "make your nice home / nice," she tells a man who is, finally, unfaithful. In "Stone Fruit," these traditional roles have become hollowed out, implicitly exploitative, as suggested by Marvin's image of a dead woman dredged from a lake—perhaps a dream image of the poet herself, *in extremis.*

Kathleen Hellen and Sharon Olds also explore the connection between capital and the objectification of women. In Hellen's "The Erotic Has No Use," the speaker's lover gives her a rare Mercury dime. The dime is "in

cardboard. Mounted," that single-word sentence suggesting sexual domi-
nation. The gift of the coin sets off a profound unease that results in the
poet's combative stance. Does the monetary exchange suggest the man's
valuation of her? In "Left-Wife Bop," Olds, who is going through a divorce,
weighs the literal and figurative value of what each partner took from the
other—including sex. She wonders "how evenly / the bounty of pleasure
fell between us— / wait, what's a bounty? Like a kidnap fee?" Surprise
shades into shock: Was sexual pleasure a way for each to kidnap the other?
The husband has been unfaithful, but the poet acknowledges that she, too,
has profited from a kind of infidelity—in her work as a poet. She writes, "I
gave my secrets / to you, dear strangers, and his, too."

Susan Briante's "Mother Is Marxist" explores motherhood and capital in
a way that destabilizes the idea of gender altogether. In Briante's formula-
tion, all of us are potentially mothers, persons who "attempt to erase the
integers, to move decimals, to point out discrepancies in the ledger, disrupt
the protocols of exchange" by which capitalist societies reduce children to
"pecuniary value." The poem is rich with historical and contemporary ex-
amples, such as the creation of child insurance during the years when child
labor was legal; the huge differences in per-pupil expenditures in public
school systems throughout the U.S.; and the warehousing of immigrant chil-
dren at the U.S. border. Such phenomena, Briante asserts, call us—mothers
of any gender in families of any constellation—to "an attitude of resistance
before the market."

The poets here explore the connection of capital and fatherhood, too,
often documenting a generational gap that both necessitates and scuttles
the possibility of father-son communication. In "Cold Calls," Edward Hirsch
speaks intimately about the experience of watching his father "dying out
there" in his quest to make money. Had we watched him do that, Hirsch
insists, we would "understand why I stood / at his grave on those wintry
afternoons . . . and raved in silence to no one." Ross White takes on a more
ambivalent father-son relationship in "Dark Money." Here, the father is in-
volved in illicit financial transactions, a bolus of fiscal corruption that drives
a wedge between him and his son.

In contrast to those living in caste societies, we here in America may dis-
pute the existence of class in our country. We may believe we are a nation
of boundless opportunity, where all people, despite the circumstances of
their birth, can be successful. After all, as Jane Hirshfield reminds us in "In

My Wallet I Carry a Card," beyond all of our affiliations and possessions—financial and otherwise—our mortality, our humanity connects us: we are of "the Order of All Who Will Die." But our poets explore also how the possession of money, or the lack of it, orients our ideas and behaviors, creating an identity and, ultimately, a cultural affiliation. In Devon Balwit's "Minding the Gap," wealth differences set individual lives on radically different trajectories. Balwit catalogs the lifestyle differences between her and her monied high-school friends. Ultimately, she says, the "doors that opened for you slammed for us." And Robert Avery's "Leisure Class" argues that class distinctions can be detected in the way some take pleasure in hard physical work—but only when it becomes a leisure activity. Such persons pick fruit, not with a laborer's bucket but, Avery writes, with a "small basket / worn like a bracelet on the forearm." Even Avery's similes point to the decorative nature of the activity. Also noteworthy here is the poet's willingness to implicate himself: the poem is in the second-person plural. This is what *we* do.

Avery's poem points to a special challenge in America, a generalized desire—whatever we may believe about the nature of class—to minimize its repercussions. We may say class exists, but that it is much more porous than in calcified old Europe, much less fixed and restraining. We want to believe that our country is a meritocracy, at least to a larger degree than other countries. Not perfect—we might say—but better. At least better. There is a reticence, a certain unseemliness, in acknowledging too much joy and identification with the money we may have. Perhaps it comes too close to embracing the kind of class identification that we, as a culture, want to reject.

A poet who, like Avery, risks such class identification is Dana Gioia. In "Shopping," Gioia owns the pleasures of having capital—even as he criticizes those pleasures. He wanders the mall, its parking lots full of "Subarus and Audis," its stores filled with "visions shining under glass, / Divinities of leather, gold, and porcelain." The poet feels the pull of these luxuries: "I am not made of stone." Ultimately, though, he finds these pleasures thin, as the poem turns toward a quest for the "fugitive," the "errant soul."

When other poets here explore the pleasure of wealth, it tends to be at an emotional remove. In "Country Club Fourth of July," Kathleen Winter records her mother "out of breath" with the unwonted luxury of the club, while the speaker herself observes the surround with a more jaundiced eye. In a poetic series, Wendy Barker complicates the pleasure of owning silver flatware and service pieces, acknowledging the brutal labor that creates such luxuries and how these items contrasted with her modest circumstances. Would it be possible, we wonder, to write a poem—one which did not alienate readers through self-congratulation—that owned and explored the pleasures of wealth in a noncritical way? Perhaps, beyond the American distrust of class association and elitism, there would simply be too high a risk of seeming smug, especially in this moment of widespread economic hardship.

On the other hand, a number of poets here document a lack of access to capital and do so to profound effect. Crystal Williams opens "Detroit as Brewster Project"—both a description of a housing project and, as the title instructs us, a simile for the entire city of Detroit—with a jarring comparison: "It must be like this in Iraq, / after a bombing." Williams immediately puts the notion of American exceptionalism on the table. If Williams's poem is outward directed, Eric Gansworth's "A Half-Life of Cardio-Pulmonary Function" portrays poverty from the inside, as he remembers growing up on a reservation. The imagery here is unsettling, even as Gansworth takes the edge off with a little humor, "clutching / a broken lacrosse stick / to intimidate rats so brazen / our housecats accepted / them as equal occupants." In "Wade Wakes Me with Sweat, Tears, and, Yes, the Rest Too," Gansworth discovers his way out, as Wade tells him to go to college. "This is truly the first time anyone," Gansworth writes, "has ever made this particular request." The line is a stark reminder: even here, in America, traditionally understood as a land of opportunity, a child might not be encouraged to pursue education as a way out of poverty—or believe that the possibility is available to him or her.

Williams addresses urban poverty. Gansworth details poverty on a reservation. Poets here take up a range of venues and experiences of need: Espada's Saint Vincent de Paul food pantry, McQuerry's yard sales, and Pratt's busker. Of course, these examples are not exhaustive. Appalachian poverty, the deprivations of the undocumented, the suburban house-poor, the homeless who live in all parts of our country: it's an ironic twist of our national diversity that we have, also, a great diversity in our poverty.

Environment and Climate

In America, we often think of land, air, and water as commodities that can be individually owned and exploited rather than collectively available. Many of the poets here remind us that such a monetary valuation of the environment is not a given—that it is, in fact, fraught and potentially dangerous. In "Money," Jane Mead demonstrates the strangeness of viewing our rivers through the lens of capital. She argues that when money intervenes, it becomes difficult to make choices that might benefit the natural world, in this case the fish inhabiting central California's Tuolumne river. Can their habitat be expanded? No—because, as Mead points out, the water "didn't belong" to them or even to itself. The given of our society suddenly seems absurd: How could either of these constituencies, both of which have an essential stake in the river, have no ownership? The title of the poem explains how. And Mark Doty's "Air Rights" reminds us that city dwellers, too, can have their access to the natural world constricted, as the one unbounded horizon left to them, sky, becomes commodified. When a neighboring building sells its air rights, Doty steps back from his ire to explore the wider implications of what's lost. If we put a price on everything, even our air, "*here* seems to thin out, / dispersed and characterless." In the auctioning of air rights, we sunder our connection to the natural world that we once owned together, that bound us.

Environmental threat also animates Xochiquetzal Candelaria's "Surrender #4: Take Notice, Take Nothing." But here, the culprit is climate change. Candelaria's poem contains images of dead bees, blasted mountains, and hurricanes, the environmental devastation wreaked by the "carnival ride" of unregulated industrialization. Perhaps the barefoot boy "danc[ing] by himself" suggests the human cost of our rabid exploitation of the natural world? Candelaria dedicates her poem "for millennials," recognizing that the generations born after the turn of the century will most acutely suffer the effects of our climate policies—policies which continue to favor quick economic return over sustainable environmental practice.

None of the speakers of these poems is an owner in the traditional capitalist sense. None paid for the natural resources whose degradation or loss motivates the poems. And yet, all are stakeholders. They have enjoyed a relationship with the natural world unmediated by money. But now, since money has intervened, the human relationship with nature is darkening, changing our relationships with one another along the way.

Looking Forward

In the years since we began working on this anthology, the distribution of capital in our country has grown more unequal, and recently enacted government policies will likely exacerbate the trend. What will result from the increasing concentration of wealth, the cannibalizing work of venture capitalism, the use of offshoring to evade national taxes, and the emphasis on stock price over salaries and benefits like health care? Where does this kind of economic manipulation lead, and what are the consequences for the people of this country? The coming of COVID-19 has only made these questions more urgent. The virus has thrown divisions among Americans into sharp relief. People of color and the urban poor, who are more likely to lack quality health care, are getting infected in far higher numbers. The roughly 40 percent of us who are able to work remotely tend to be white and middle class. Pandemic-related school closings have made it difficult or impossible for millions of children to receive the subsidized school meals they need to stave off hunger. And when it comes to the distribution of federal aid, many mom-and-pop businesses have gone without while much money has gone to larger companies with little immediate need, leading some to return those funds when their disbursement became known.

The long-term repercussions of the pandemic's economic shock are hard to project. What is richly apparent is that, in the coming years, Americans will be faced with political decisions that ask us to consider how to move on from this moment. Will we relaunch the country on a more secure, environmentally sustainable, and socially equitable path? Even now, ideas once seemed marginal are being brought to the table, such as universal basic income, universal health care, and large-scale, publicly funded work projects. In this moment of upheaval, we will be asking ourselves, what do we want our nation to be?

Finding answers to such questions won't be easy; democracy is messy. But we believe poetry can help us see what's at stake. Poems require no special materials to produce and, in these days of new media, are relatively simple to share. As a result, poetry can rise above the forces of the marketplace, offering us truths often obscured by our polarized politics and siloed media. The voices of the poets in this volume range from the intimate to the insistent, the compassionate to the challenging. Taken together, they present a broad vision of American capitalism as a shaping force in our lives—a *necessary* vision as we decide, together, who we want to be.

CLARE ROSSINI AND BENJAMIN S. GROSSBERG
August 2020

The Poetry
of Capital

Alan Chazaro

Alan Chazaro is the author of *This Is Not a Frank Ocean Cover Album* (Black Lawrence Press, 2018) and *Piñata Theory* (Black Lawrence Press, 2020). A Lawrence Ferlinghetti Fellow from the University of San Francisco, his poems have appeared in *Ninth Letter*, *San Francisco Chronicle*, *Puetro Del Sol*, and *Iron Horse Review*.

∿ *El Paletero's Song*

each flame-throwing summer
we'd stay in a pool of air-
conditioned cool until he called

Paletas!

his voice the graffiti
braiding fences
around our neighborhood

Tengo paletas!

sugar melody rising
above noises from
the nearby freeway

Paletas de Piña!

our ice-cream-man
wheeling what we wanted
across sticky pavement

Paletas de Limon!

handcart plastered with pictures
of Spider-Man popsicles
with blue gumballs for eyes

Paletas de Cacahuate!

chased around street corners
by little ones, kids
with missing teeth

Paletas de Fresa!

handing out fruit pops
in exchange for smiles
and crinkled dollar bills

Paletas de Tamarindo!

bundling money in his back-
pocket with rubber bands
because no one carried his interest

Paletas de Arroz!

stopping only to wipe sweat
off his sun-glazed brow
before pushing on

Paletas de Mango!

a cowboy in leather boots
circling suburban blocks
until he gathered enough savings

Paletas!

who showed us photos
of his family in Jalisco, three
boys and a wife he left

∽ The Cowboy Shirts

He was secreted North
so he could own a Chevy
and drive over paved roads.

To his wife and five kids
in Mexico he flickered
until fading. Nothing

but his side of the mattress and
some extra plates to remind them
a father once lived there.

In California he worked
under the table, a cash-
only laborer. He married

our grandma, an American
native, her skin as dark
and leathery as a bargain purse.

He didn't speak English,
didn't know what his name
meant: *Fortunato.*

A *borracho.*
Could build a wall a week
after he tore the old ones down.

And a gambler, out late nights
with the guys in the back shed,
smoking and singing and pissing

on grass he mowed that after-
noon. Mornings, he would stumble
home with sex and tequila

on his mustache, barking
why isn't breakfast ready?
He was lucky: *Fortunato.*

Bragged about the time he punched
an officer, only to be bailed
out of jail by a woman.

Once, when he upset grandma—
like often, like oceans—
we threatened

to call Immigration.
But how could we—
the children of immigrants

ourselves?
We didn't want him living
in our house.

At our parties. Using
our toilets, our hand soap.
One night when he went

out drinking, our cousin
crouched over a pile
of clothes inside his room

and pissed, an unofficial
send-off. For months his shirt
collars stunk of her urine.

From the Poet

Growing up as a first-generation Mexican American has given me the abil-
ity to navigate a range of environments, from the richest areas of San Fran-
cisco to the poorest neighborhoods of Mexico. Though I was raised with the
privileges of a California middle-class family, many of my friends and
neighbors were without the advantages that most Americans have long
taken for granted, even in a time of crisis—those advantages bestowed by
U.S. citizenship. My background has allowed me to learn from those on all
points of the economic spectrum. I've seen how many people have always
had to work twice as hard to get half as much. My poems are about some
of the undocumented immigrants I've lived with or known throughout
my life as friends—about their sacrifices and victories, their struggles
and sometimes their flaws. Immigrants constitute an essential part of our
country's workforce, yet the average American doesn't have much knowl-
edge of their daily existence beyond seeing them serve in restaurants or
clean an office building.

And now, in the age of COVID-19, that word "essential" has taken on
new meaning. Who are the ones who are essential in keeping this country
operational? Who comes to your mind? Who is preparing your food, pack-
ing your meat, working at the grocery store, taking care of your children,
wiping down tables, keeping customers six feet apart? Immigrants make
up a large portion of this nation's essential workforce, yet how often do we
give them the economic and social dignity they deserve for their contribu-
tions? I want to bring this community and their reality to the attention of
readers. For anyone who doesn't live in a neighborhood full of diverse and
immigrant *paleteros*, restaurant workers, mechanics, landscapers, and con-
struction workers—and so can escape the reality of their hard labor—my
hope is that these poems can bring a different perspective on the value of
work, money, family, and freedom in America.

Aricka Foreman

Aricka Foreman is a poet, essayist, and digital curator from Detroit,
Michigan. Author of *Dream with a Glass Chamber* (YesYes Books, 2016)
and *Salt Body Shimmer* (YesYes Books, 2020), she has received fellowships
from Cave Canem, Callaloo, and the Millay Colony for the Arts. Her work
has appeared in *RHINO, Buzzfeed, James Franco Review, THRUSH,*
and *Furious Flower: Seeding the Future of African American Poetry*
(Northwestern University Press, 2019). She spends her time in
Chicago, experimenting with photography and video-narratives.

⤳ Still Life of Acme in Spring
for francine, for Detroit

From my mouth, forgive me: friend, woman.
When I said there are no flowers here, I forgot
to mention the bloom of lace around a young girl's

ankle at Easter, her peony-shaped afro puffs,
the carnelian carnations pinned to dresses to honor
mothers not lost. Spectrum of May collected from

Eastern Market, rowed in mismatched rainbows
in red wagons or inside the phantom box of a son's
arms. I forget the cured meat spread out from the black

barrel of a barbeque, bushel of yarn sopped with sauce,
unlike the gauze full of blood from a young boy's head.
Dear God the plankton of music dying our faces in the hot

summer streets, fever of jazz, blush of blues: raw heart
confront me. This city, always in my face. Bouquet of
incense, apothecaries with shea and oils. Give a dollar

and I'll show you a conductor, his white bucket symphony.
No I haven't forgotten the fire, molotov shards spreading
orange and gold flames as a field of dahlia across our

living room licking my mother's heels, the heroine wolf
dragging me from my bed. I don't blame the addict
who didn't know which house to huff and blow down,

or the firemen arriving late. And yes, angels too.
A neighbor who let me, knees pressed to sternum, watch
from his porch as our house ashed itself clean. We have

to see the truth of things. Did I say there was no flora here?
No pollen shaken from the anther's round head?
The yellow dust settling in the cracks of windshield?
I meant: give me a plot. I'll dig to the rich black.

～ Price of Today's Ticket

Quarters from a Coinstar receipt:
canned tuna, fresh dill. Crock-
pot miracles of beans, roots

seasonally cheap. For ramen,
half-dozen eggs, chives,
handful of greens. Bread

for the pantry supply of peanut
butter, eggs again over-easy,
scrambled, or poached if I want

to get real middle class. An apple,
or one pear, though, when the empty
in me tries at the grainy meat, I forget

what little regard I have for the fruit
except what it can do for me. Could I
be more American or more idealistic,

buying books instead of dinner? A pound
of coffee can warm my belly for a week.
If there are few things more rude

than discussing money or politics over
dinner, you must've been unimpressed
with the fat on your tables. Where I come

from a scraped-fork is a praise song
of turning nothing into some-exquisite-
thing licked clean from the finger.

～ Before I Fire Her, the Therapist Asks What IS It Like to Be a Black Woman HERE: A Monologue
after Ross Gay

I love your hair You always wear such *interesting* things What did you do
before this Wow are you from Detroit What was that like Tell me what
your thesis is about That sounds really powerful Your poem tonight was

really intense You'll appreciate this, you know, since you're kind of ghetto
You worked so hard you made it So what did you think about that Junot
essay I'm suspicious of poems with an agenda, that have a certain
aboutness Explain what you mean when you say risk I'm really
uncomfortable I went to Detroit, well Dearborn, and it's amazing how
cheap the houses are No, it's a really cool town Are you a Tigers fan That
city is having a hard time, for sure I lived there once when I worked for
Teach for America How do you feel about people who claim Detroit but
aren't really from there I really love your hair Is your work always so
intense That line is a little melodramatic I'm not as smart as you but I
thought rape was about sex What do you mean it's hard to date I mean
you're *here* Rap is about music let's not make it about race Oh come on,
I only call people I love my nigger I don't mean this to sound racist but
You don't seem like you date white guys but I love how our skin looks
when I hold your hand and I like women who live a natural lifestyle and
You're so well spoken Wow you've really read a lot Ithaca must be way
different than what you're used to You can breathe now, you made it

ᔕ *October*

Thicket of auburn and gold scattered
across old railroad tracks. Rain
spreads its thin net over fallen trunks
hollow with rot, feeble roots: even nature
has given up and let go. I run, though these legs
must learn again the muscle's music, red air
stretching every ligament and tendon,
past the bison farm, those sad-eyed blue-tagged
darlings flicker as I rustle up what is dead or dying.
Throat burns where there has been no water for
weeks. I call up your name and cough, lungs
shake loose a flora of tar, brine of whiskey.
This town still too lush with new, I want to go
back to the city where I loved you, sweat to the steady
pulse of house, pluck and strum of our guitars in the late
hours. I want to run the streets where we smoked
and talked shit, bellow against what fails us:

overgrown plots, overdrawn accounts when we
needed to eat most, bargain our way beneath the roofs
over our heads. Streets that taught us how to grind,
what hustle is made of: our names and insomniac nights,
belief in the gods of potluck, of good will and favors,
me running toward the arms that will not let us starve,
toward the porches after Sunday dinner, and when one
of us dies, to hold us and pour another glass.
When I say fall, perhaps I mean: to come down
from a high place, from the throne of garage band
albums, the cloud of bardic hymns, or maybe
something as simple as you standing above, me
curled into a knot in my bed, among the ruins
of stray clothes and dogeared books, empty
cartons of cigarettes. I run against the branches
that whip and raise the skin. Run until the salt
stains, the heart gives in, run until the wheeze
carves out each letter of you that is left, until what
is left cramps and seizes. Submits to its undoing.

From the Poet

Somehow I keep circling back to the idea of compromise when I think of
capital in this country and this art. As in: I *compromise* sleep in order to
work, to pay rent and gas and a cellphone bill. What's said of the poor writer
is that the writer will die poor. What's said of the poor writer is that they
were dreamers. What's said of the poor writer (while they're living) is not
about their dream—or, if it is about their dream, it is just that, a dream,
nothing real. The dream is often less valuable unless its service can be jus-
tified. Poets who are also educators are socially valued more than, say, poets
who work in service, hourly positions. In this COVID-19 moment, these
service-poets are deemed essential. And educators are deemed less, save for
the virtue signaling that fails to close the gap of adjunct versus tenure and
doesn't account for the institutional hierarchies that determine who has the
right to support themselves in a capitalistic system.

What does poetry of capital mean in light of the classist models of genre,
often marketed toward the MFA? Or, if poetry is occasional enough to traffic
in Black, Brown, Queer, Trans, GNC trauma: then used for a conference, a

festival, a workshop. In Immigrant trauma in response to the horrific conditions at our borders, having been forgotten or smoldered in the wake of current necessary rebellions. In our Indigenous communities' trauma when a new anthology comes along. In drug-addicted trauma, which for many is also the trauma of being poor. We can really do this all day.

I'm lucky. I have a community of writers, colleagues: Other'd. Who say, too: "I'm tired," but it's not as despondent as it seems. Or it is. We're all tired. If all of us are tired, how do we resist bringing that tired into poems, into essays, into reviews, into reading submissions? How does that serve this Poetry Machine, some announcing every other season its death. As I write this, the old, violent Americana nuts and bolts of the Poetry Machine are being shaken loose. And I want to think clearly about what we make in its place for the generation of poets after us. What possibilities we can build conspicuously in its place.

I can't say that my thinking is right or the only way. I try to be thoughtful and honest when I say: I have questions. At heart, I'm a Black femme from Detroit insistent on not believing everything I hear, and side-eyeing everything that sounds like a script. Sometimes I get caught up in the possibility that we can be better. And maybe that's the push I want from my work, from the work I read, from the work I hope to support and foster. In the voices that say, "Burn the orchard clean."

I don't have a neat answer, but I have these poems, alive in the moment, that ask what they need to ask to get to the next question. Maybe that's not transactional. But about rigor. And a deep desire to protect the imagination. We might want to sit down a long while, to think about it, to take a deep-body-sigh and evaluate. Radically demand something, dare I say, different.

We plant something new.

Claire McQuerry

Claire McQuerry's collection *Lacemakers* won the 2010
Crab Orchard First Book Prize in Poetry, and her poems have appeared
in *Tin House, Poetry Northwest, Fugue,* and *American Literary Review.*
She is an assistant professor at Bradley University in Illinois.

∾ Textbook Ekphrasis

1. Figure 2.7, "The Business Cycle"

Small as a halved credit card,
inked in cool tones, the figure's waves trace
output over time. The green arrows, *recession*,
descend to troughs, while *recovery* lifts to crests of pale blue—

these the blah, soothing hues of the dentist's office
in which a patient gazes at the ceiling, knowing
certain shining instruments on a tray behind her chair
will soon be in the dentist's hands.

Otherwise, the page is text-dense and colorless.
So generic, so stripped down, those plotted curves
could just as well measure air currents
or weather fronts.

    If you wonder whether weather

will affect the cycle, yes, it will. You can
read it in a sidebar—*weather
or wars or other external forces.*

Compress these winds to a figure then.
    Render them
mute. The graph bears no sine wave
of sadness, no plot points of emptied

rooms, though I imagine the ghost of those
indicators, at an inverse to the ones we see.

> The hurricane turned the air
> to static, to fan
> blades—neighborhoods
> flayed to the scaffolds.
>
> Survivors warmed canned meats
> on propane stoves, in
> temporary shelters.

Example 3a: external factors

Depression

Grandmother, never one to go on
about herself, mentioned her youth only in passing—

> Bread lines, stitches, a row
> house, everything in rows.

Figure 6: recovered

apart from the single story she'd relate, even when
memory had receded to floss:

Manhattan had no need for artists then.
I'd wait in lines for hours, in dark hallways, in clouds of smoke—
my portfolio under one arm, a hundred others ahead of me.

The story ends when she runs out of money, settles
on a secretary job and marries a drunk. About the job,
it was *nice* she'd always insisted.

She would finish, and forget she'd told me, and begin again
Manhattan had no need for artists then. . . .

Recession

Yet, the story of every life
is a long series of disappointments.
What person could say she's happy every day? Even so—

what became of all those paintings grandmother
never painted? Do they exist in some dim
gallery of another, possible world?

On the street, one woman tells her friend, *The life I'm living now*
is not the one I planned. And the friend:
So true. This is not the narrative I'd been given.

The first crocuses open like pocketknives on the lawns of the city,
in the bald mud of ice-wasted
plots. Compromise
and revision—

compromise, and sometimes surrender.

> I go to my neighbor's tag sale.
> Inside, her house looks ordinary—
> apart from the prices on everything,
> even the toaster, coats
> in the closet. *Should cover another*
> *month's rent*, she says, and unplugs
> the fringed lamp she just sold. I too
> am almost broke. I buy a flower pot for 50 cents.
> When I come by next morning, she has nothing
> left to sell. Her footfalls
> ring out loudly as she crosses
> the empty rooms.

Example 3

And yet, I wanted to get dressed up,
go out in sequined blouses and get
a buzz, until I felt all the potential selves
beating there, at the ends of my nerves,
a bonus door, behind which
I might find the hidden prize.

Grandmother would.
She'd hold cocktails like gem-encrusted
goblets, flourishing her cigarettes
because they did that, in the films of her youth,
those women who got what they wanted, who
had arrived somewhere.

Later, at the lowest,
a two-dollar beer's an extravagance.
My friend ate only oatmeal for months. Even
the sequins were gone.

Recovery

And I read today the economy's on the mend. Remarkable
textbook recovery.

Except for all that's irrevocable—

the debts, the break-up, the watch that's pawned
to pay a bill. Go back for it later
and it's already gone. Little
humiliating subtractions.

Those lines on a graph.
So detached. And yet

the whole country, the world,
rides them like sea swells.

When grandmother took me to the Red Cottage Buffet,
she'd slide butter pats, packaged saccharine,
single-serving creamers into a Ziplock in her purse. *You never know,*
she'd say, *where your next lunch is gonna come from, Sugar,*
and lay her napkin, then, ceremoniously across her lap.

Figure 15

From the Poet

Just after the last economic collapse, in 2008, I found myself without a job
and struggling to pay the bills. Even my application to work for a maid ser-
vice was rejected. After several miserable months, when I was down to
nothing in my bank account, I got a miracle job offer, through a friend of a
friend, to work as a ghostwriter for a textbook company. That experience
inspired "Textbook Ekphrasis" as well as a related manuscript of poems.

The ghostwriting job was the strangest and worst job of my life. Every
two weeks, the textbook "authors" would send me an outline of the chapter
they wanted me to write—on topics from cinema to economics to sales and
marketing—with the expectation that I would then "borrow" content from
whatever other sources I could find to flesh out the chapter. Not only were

the ethics of this practice fairly questionable, but I was disturbed by some of the content itself. The book on sales and marketing, for instance, took the stance that every human interaction involves a kind of sales pitch. People were not people but "prospects" or "customers." There was also the irony that I was writing, in a very basic, textbooky way, about things like economic recession and fiscal policy, even as—in fact *because*—these issues were having a real and immediate impact on my own life. I couldn't quit my job because there were no other jobs to be had. In fact, I felt luckier than a lot of my friends who were in more desperate straits and had to move back in with parents or sometimes go without food.

I was finally able to quit when I got accepted to a PhD program in English a year later. Though my boss told me when I left that I was throwing my life away, I knew that her statement couldn't be further from the truth. My year of ghostwriting helped me see that our responsibility to one another begins in language, the way we represent reality. The economic collapse that left so many without homes, or jobs, or dignity, was the result of a greed and corruption that could only succeed by turning human beings into abstractions—specifically, equating persons with profit. Choosing to write and study poetry felt like an antidote to the thing I *had* been doing with words because, of course, poetry works in the opposite direction: it renders human beings in particulars, and it invites us to empathize. This feels only more necessary now as we face another, more devastating economic collapse, and the pressure to ignore human welfare for corporate profit feels louder and more explicit than ever.

Will Cordeiro

Will Cordeiro's collection *Trap Street* (Able Muse Press, 2020)
won the 2019 Able Muse Book Award. His work has appeared in *Agni*,
Cimarron Review, *The Cincinnati Review*, *The Threepenny Review*, and
elsewhere. He coedits Eggtooth Editions and teaches in the
Honors College at Northern Arizona University.

∾ Piecework

Six o'clock, before the heat-stroke
highs that summer, I'd start to crawl
through dusty clouds of gnats, between
the narrow divots separating bells from
habaneros, belly down upon my hands
and knees to the horizon. Some rotten
spot would burst, pulp spurting—
popping seeds. I'd brush the smutch off
on my jeans, wipe my brow, and spit
a loogy; itch my neck, then—without
fail—raw juice would make its way
into my eyes. Bright, fluid, loose. . . .
Dirt-glazed, I'd blink it back then ball
my fists into my sockets, a trick which
only seemed to rub it in. I'd twist
my T-shirt up to mop my face,
squinting at the blood-crazed sun,
praying it'd stop before I stooped back
down to suffer another half a bushel.
I'd daydream while the others labored,
migrants making cracks in Spanish
or the old poor blacks who arrived
earlier than me, their quick sure hands
hustling while my scrawny ass just
shuffled and whittle-picked along—
and I'd think god, fuck it, at least
for me it's only a crummy summer
job, at least I'll cut out soon, done
by lunch. By nine o'clock, hungry,
I'd hate my life; I'd loop back around
the rows. I'd vow never to return,
since, hell, the pittance in my pocket
vanished through a hole. I cussed
my parents for forcing me to learn
what they termed "the value of work."
Still, another dawn, I'd wake up stiff,

a broken thing, gut it out, swill instant
coffee, grit and all, then go to squat
in fields again. I'd toil over every line
of ripened plants with rotten visions
it'd never end—I didn't plan to stay
fourteen, and yet each noon I'd count
my haul, each basketful along its rut,
my skin alive with every fiery thing.

 ∾ Smoke

Or all that it's become departs across
a river's scum as if on an assembly line.
Winter dusk and factories hush. Stacks

silhouette into the lockdown sentinels
that guard us here. At five o'clock, sunk
sun guts roughhewn brick, a lush high

residue burns out the air's arrested
hue borne over a city's bottlenecks
and mottles it to molten bric-a-brac.

Rundown, overrun with invasive skunk
grass, parks sink in rubble. A kid jerks
see-saws and screws on a scruffy jungle

gym. Swings get tangled and weed-lots
lace with shards of glass. Sprayed tags
penumbra. Stubbled faces turn away—

they hurry on, crisscrossed by the chain
links. I pass men wrinkled, rankled, laid
off, outsourced, thrown out with a pink

slip. Give me the bounty, the soil's yield
into this river, its riven backwash riddled
by our refineries until it might catch fire.

I am annealed. Night-walk me past these
staggered blocks, warped docks and slag
-heaps, oil barrels, byways littered in rags.

Feel bloodlines draining down each blade
of grass made greener in the runoff's slop.
I hitch the beltway with you past my pit-

stop—then bang!—into a flophouse, flap-
jack flat and folded up, and I am straddled
between staying and asking you to take me

with you. I'd just be some spit-out hanger
-on, I know. You're bent for one last slow
drag before blowing out a ring of nothing.

∿ Spambot

Within the cloud, your data's porridge.
The technocrats will mine your answers
Until the background's noise
Best fits the dashed-off lines they'd give us.

In cyberspace, we're each a tourist.
Capitalism = our happy cancer.
So what's your beef? The choice
Is yours. We're born carnivorous. . . .

Go work your butt off and you'll feel
Like ass. No money down; more girls on top.
Don't opt out or you'd stop to think.
Dream big. Take stock. Sleep in. Get smashed.

Reinvent a new revolving wheel.
Take your pick of clickbait—and your drive's corrupt.
Mind's full of junk, a viral jinx.
Now render back to seizure all your cash.

From the Poet

Poetry creates value. But the values of poetry are rarely the values of the marketplace.

In the first chapter of *Walden*, Thoreau tells a parable of a basket-weaver who envies a lawyer. The lawyer "had only to weave arguments, and, by some magic, wealth and standing followed." The lawyer refuses to buy the basket-weaver's wares, and the basket-weaver walks off disgusted. Thoreau claims he, too, is a weaver—of tales. And yet he does not study how to sell his goods profitably, but rather how to "avoid the necessity of selling them." Thoreau wishes to live by his own system of values, outside the marketplace.

Material things pass into dust. But poetry returns infinite dividends; it is passed on.

Diogenes reportedly once said, "I have come to debase the coinage." A coin is only a placeholder with negligible intrinsic value. Diogenes also said, "In the rich man's house there's nowhere to spit but in his face." To debase the coinage is thus to challenge such authority, to question the practices and tacit faith that undergird the scheme by which things, words, and ideas are commonly exchanged.

Metaphors, too, are an exchange: a carrying over, a transfer. They debase conventional meanings. They substitute the instabilities of figuration for the going-rate of literal correspondence. Metaphors reveal, through the significance they forge, that matter-of-fact signification itself is potentially counterfeit. Ultimate value is still up for negotiation.

All language is metaphor, dead or alive. And the liveliest, most electric metaphors raise the specter that the seeming-solid ground beneath our feet is actually shifting and fecund and may resurrect with untold multitudes.

Judging the weight and measure of words, poets learn an economy apart from the coin of the realm. It is not words alone—rhythm and tone, mouthfeel and pitch—that they measure and weigh. It is the worlds contained within and the visions by which those worlds are perceived. Poets take the measure of weights and measures. Poets tip the scales or tear the scales from our eyes.

Poetry pays us back by making us pay attention.

Thoreau's cabin sits not in some isolated wilderness but adjacent to the railroad tracks and a short walk from his mother's house. She did his laundry for him. He had a quid pro quo with Emerson, who had become relatively wealthy through his writing. Emerson allowed Thoreau to stay on his land in exchange for improving it.

Black markets, gift economies, poetic economies, official markets—all operate side-by-side, spliced and plaited, co-dependent and imbricated. The contradictions of capital are legion.

No one owns a language, at least. Still, poetry is a pilfering that boosts from our common wordhoard. We read during stolen hours. Our inheritance must be earned anew.

Anne Carson reminds us that the quick-witted and wandering Odysseus earned the epithet, "the one who profits."

How does poetry enrich us?

Ross White

Ross White is the author of *Charm Offensive*, winner of the 2019
Sexton Prize, and two chapbooks. He is the director of Bull City Press,
an independent publisher of poetry, fiction, and nonfiction, and the editor
of *Four Way Review*. He teaches creative writing and grammar at the
University of North Carolina at Chapel Hill and is the associate director
of The Frost Place Conference on Poetry. His poems have appeared
in *American Poetry Review*, *New England Review*, *Poetry Daily*,
Tin House, and *The Southern Review*, among others.

◕ *Savings & Loan*

> We see Occupy Wall Street protestors crying out for an America that
> lets all of us reach for the American Dream again—a dream that says
> if you work hard and play by the rules, you can have a good life and
> retire with dignity.
>
> —John Garamendi

Occupy the late 1980s. Occupy my parents'
contentious divorce, the frozen joint account.
Occupy every other weekend. Occupy
the long car rides with my father, dialing
his own answering machine from the car phone
to leave messages for himself. Occupy
the crushing boredom he must have felt
driving me across Maryland, Delaware,
northern Virginia on Saturday afternoons,
without real destinations in mind.
Occupy the National Bank of Washington
on Sunday mornings, tugging at bronze
chains to light bent green desk lamps,
tiny under the Florentine chandelier
of its titanic lobby, the Renaissance grandeur
of its sandstone and hand-painted trim.
Money breathed life into my father.
He push-pinned new branch locations into city maps
with the care of a Caravaggio.
So many more temples to transactionality.
In the quiet of money, he would work
and I would kneel before the polished steel
vault door or skip behind the teller counters.
All week he must have waited to be alone
in the presence of money. He must have hated
to share it with me every odd weekend,
but I was nothing if not reverent.
My mother told me it was impolite
to talk about money, so I never told anyone
about the dark silver wheel of the vault door,
the stale smell of sitting currency.

I never asked questions. The regulators
in dark suits came to the house
one night. I never asked questions.
My father moved into an efficiency
apartment, researched spousal privilege.
I never asked questions. He seemed spent
by money, though money was his occupation.
It was all that could occupy him.

∿ Dark Money

Of all lies, the worst is *The truth will set you free.*
I don't think truth unshackled my father.
Truth paid his moving expenses, set him up
in his grandmother's house with his new wife—
his former secretary—and two children he didn't know
how to talk to. Truth banished him
from branch location and operations,
from belonging to the fraternity of money,
and in his exile, he wandered by motorcycle
from flea market to gun show.
In twenty-five years since, I don't think truth
has, like a magician, swept doves from under
its handkerchiefs, or doubled my father's joints
to free him from the straitjacket and cuffs.
He collects badges. Detectives, marshals,
the old silver stars. He still believes in law
and order, even as the television he keeps muted
shows him images of protestors, of the officers
who discharged weapons into unarmed teens.
Has it brought him any comfort to know
where the money came from, whose pockets
it now lines? Has it brought him any comfort
to speak that truth to regulators? Sometimes
in my dreams, I see the Keating Five seated
in a circle, cigars and good Scotch, in a dim room.
They laugh about dark money, having taken

so much out in the open, and John Glenn says,
I could still go back into space, and John McCain says,
Who knows? Maybe I'll just run for President,
and then they both do—
                              but, before—
my father shuffles in, his expression neutral,
a white cloth draped over his arm,
puts their empties on his tray, and asks
if there's anything else he can do for them.

From the Poet

When I was growing up, my family didn't talk about money. My parents considered it impolite.

My father was an Executive Vice President for the National Bank of Washington.

But my family didn't talk about money. My parents considered it impolite.

Federal regulators seized control of NBW, the District of Columbia's oldest financial institution, on August 1, 1990. After years of risky real estate lending, the bank finally declared bankruptcy from its creditors, and a flurry of indictments followed. My father's boss, Luther H. Hodges, Jr., a man who had cast a long shadow over my childhood when my father followed him from the North Carolina National Bank to NBW, surrendered the chairmanship of the bank he partly owned and moved to New Mexico. A new flurry of indictments followed, charging the directors and numerous bank executives with mismanagement and malfeasance. One of the executives my parents regularly invited to family dinners committed suicide before the suit was settled. My father returned to North Carolina, moved into his grandmother's house, and began a new career in real estate appraisal. He never returned to banking.

Even after that, my family didn't talk about money. We still don't.

Diana Marie Delgado

Diana Marie Delgado is the author of *Tracing the Horse* (BOA Editions, 2019) and the chapbook *Late Night Talks with Men I Think I Trust* (Center for the Book Arts, 2015). She is the recipient of numerous grants, including a fellowship from the National Endowment for the Arts. A graduate of Columbia University, she currently resides in Tucson, where she is the Literary Director of the Poetry Center at the University of Arizona.

ᵔᵔ *Free Cheese and Butter*

Mom's good at waiting.
We can stand for hours

but she won't tie and untie
shoelaces like my brother

who yanks pigtails and pinches
with monkey hands,

that smell of sweaty nickels.
I practice her signature in the air,

a clump of curlicues,
all the round letters of the alphabet.

My brother tugs my arm,
points to the end of the line.

Patty Garcia's there with
teeth like the keys

on Mr. Sergio's piano, eyes
so big she blinks a lot

to keep them in. At school,
she's who we chase.

ᵔᵔ *Man of the House*

My brother brings home diamonds

Mom scratches against
the coffee table glass.

I'm on the couch, reading *The Stand*

when he walks in after stealing
a woman's purse.

Later, I watch him wrap
a shotgun in a blanket,

place it in the trunk
of Danny's car.

Dad, from the bedroom:

Who does he think he is
bringing home finery?

～ La Puente

Letter from Corcoran Prison: Please deposit $1,500 into the P.O. Box
    of Debra C.—the Mafia's going to kill me.

After 9/11 they asked the Chicanos in prison and one of them raised
    his hand: How do you think we took it? We're Americans.

Mule Creek, Delano, Chowchilla, Avenal, Pelican Bay, Calipatria,
    Centinela, Ironwood, Solano, Wasco, Corcoran, Tehachapi.

California has a lot of prisons, all with beautiful names.

A cop I'm dating charges a gang member with possession: I
    understand you—the people I arrest remind me of your family.

Dad's arm out the car window: You're going to have a hard time
    finding a man.

On my brother's 40th birthday: I played gin rummy with Birdman.
    Manson's worth money, the court signs his name with a stamp.

After robbing H&H Liquor, drowsy with blood, they hide in the
    cellar, and dream the same thing: gang fame.

Driving to the methadone clinic: You know too much about us.
    Addicts are lucky: they get to focus on one thing their entire life.

Dad's drunk: Cornell, Princeton, Pepperdine? The names sound like
    exotic spices! Where you going to?

On a bench at La Puente Park: Call my manager—he stashed ten thousand
    for me. From his backpack he pulls a dead watch.

I lived next to a train crossing on Valley Blvd, the sky above pink-
and-gold stars.

Summers were horses traced on denim; my youth unfolding,
paper fan.

From the Poet

There's a counterculture, often ignored, that exists in many communities
of color. Economics places us on the margins. It pushes us to make deci-
sions we wouldn't make if we had opportunities—if we had a way to hope.
Most Americans assume that we all have equal opportunity and a path for-
ward. But from what I've seen, that's just not true.

These poems, taken from my book *Tracing the Horse*, emerge from an
impulse to explore the psychology behind the choices made by those who
are most economically disenfranchised.

Growing up, I saw needy families, including my own, resort to selling
drugs and stealing. Of course, I was urged not to do these kinds of things,
but I witnessed them happening all around me—it was how people sur-
vived. We were the working poor, never able to take for granted the basics,
such as food, clothes, and a home. We waited in line at the community
center for free cheese, government pork, and big blocks of butter. Our life
was often bare bones.

These poems attempt to reveal the motivations behind what we do and
how we behave when we don't have enough. In "Free Cheese and Butter,"
I tried to evoke how childhood hierarchies prevail even when families are
in line to receive food assistance. And "Man of the House" describes my
brother coming home and sharing the spoils of a robbery; at the time, I
felt a strong competition emerge, as if my brother was outshining my dad.
I found this conflict really upsetting, but also interesting, and I tried to
tease out the subtext of this interaction to reveal what ultimately is a family
dynamic rooted in survival.

Xochiquetzal Candelaria

Xochiquetzal Candelaria's *Empire* was published in 2011 by the
University of Arizona Press. Her work has appeared in *The Nation*,
New England Review, *Gulf Coast*, and *Seneca Review*, and she has
received fellowships from the Bread Loaf Writers' Conference and the
National Endowment for the Arts. Candelaria is currently a
professor at the City College of San Francisco.

∿ Surrender #4: Take Notice, Take Nothing
for millennials

Residue of radioactive salt
streaked along the counter.

She starts to gather dead bees
before her eyes burn and tear

as the wreckage cools. . . .
We line up, we wait . . .

for the carnival ride to begin spinning again.

How long have we been blasting
the buzzing mountains?

The dark?

New buildings lean toward the sea

(an optical illusion some say)

like peace, democracy.

We used to think
in terms of moving on.

Now the train station might as well be a hospital ward
where a barefoot boy dances by himself
at the end of the platform.

But even before this,
there were signs

of compressed heat,
an absence in the swell.

Did they tell us to sell the parks,
libraries, estuaries?

Did they tell us our lives
were best kept private

so we wouldn't be missed?

Did legislators pawn the dawn
and the signature of trees,

and did we openly greet
hurricanes,

name them: Cindy, Susan, Sheryl-Anne
as if we could sexualize what we had tampered with?

What about a night so clear,
a milk so blue?

Fresh bread, steam spreading
the smell of butter and tomato,

a chair made by a father
and kept for a great, great grandchild?

A pair of worn brown shoes at the threshold.

∿ Matter

It matters that the young ones slept on the marble steps all night
                                        to keep the school open,
reached for each other's   cold numb hands
                              for the first time, heat rising in their hungry
                              stomachs.
Someone runs to get burritos   and through the din of sirens
                                     and barricades
does not return. Nothing and everything matters   when the
    matter is money.
Their bodies are money,
        their bodies debt. *I owe everything to the stars
                and moss-covered rocks*
outside the main library I overheard one of them say once
                              in a poem never written down,
so never burned in the pyre
                started by a group that was paid ten dollars an hour
                        and promised Subway sandwiches.

In the fourth book on forgiveness,
      the young lovers are exhausted,
            their salty bodies swollen and resting,
their bright eyes closed as if to say, please do not call
          this pornography, please
remember all lives together
        are one body   ablaze.

∼ Boom

I wake up as rabbits; nothing but fur
against fur, a rabbit in ruins, twin spires

of my ears eavesdropping on conversations,

the asymptote of me forever rising, forever
falling, offering myself at

market in exchange for fare.

I burrow below the Treasury Building,
chomping on silver shavings, glowing E

Pluribus Unum at night

(dreaming of my cousin

of haute couture lying
against a woman's back,

my matted sister, skinned brother),
glistening like Dubai silk on

LCD billboards tracking homes,
begotten like rabbits but never built.

From the Poet

Recently a close friend told me that she believed collective loving conscious-
ness was needed before we could implement coordinated action to address
global-warming-induced fires, homelessness, and children in cages at the
border. After I hung up, I realized that I write poems because I don't have

to wait for ethical consciousness to precede action. Writing poems can develop ethical consciousness and *is* action.

After the fall of the Soviet Union, my father lamented that without an oppositional force, U.S. capitalism no longer had to play nice, no longer had to rein in the greedy mechanisms by which it runs. For goods to be sold, we have to believe that we are always lacking something. This is what capitalism tells us. To me, poems do the opposite. Poems affirm our wholeness even in the face of loss. This is not to say that real world plights do not need solutions, but rather, that unchecked capitalism creates problems that are not real and denies problems that are.

In the poem "Take Notice, Take Nothing," I chronicle the way in which, if things remain the same, we are headed toward a functionless society. I try to give shape to the problem the current economic and political model presents, many of which became more insistent, more unavoidable in the face of the COVID-19 pandemic. However, the poem ends with an image of boots that symbolize both work and rest simultaneously. The image is meant to give us hope: we know how to work with integrity, and we need to do so now more than ever.

Yes, I am angry about the state of the world today, but when I write, I feel connected to a long-standing, coordinated effort to honor the ephemeral, the delicate, the complex, the song. In "Matter," the lovers meet because they are trying to oppose austerity. I implicate the reader at the end because I want the reader to value the young people but also to recognize that we as Americans are primed to see the young as entertainment. The speaker of the poem turns directly to the reader and asks him/her/they not to commodify the lovers.

I have two small children, and so the devastation of our moment and how it will affect the future are intimate concerns. Unchecked capitalism does not promote connection, rest, or work (strangely). To me it is the embodiment of restlessness.

My hope is that when people read these poems, they feel their physical relationship to the landscape and their deep emotional need for connection. Our anger has a lot of power, and underneath the anger is love that has no channel, no conduit to move through. If capitalism is about restlessness, my poems are about movement. By detailing all the ways we get stuck, I want to carve out a space for the love to rage, eddy, bound, and heal.

Robert Avery

Robert Avery is a teacher from Bucks County, Pennsylvania.
His poetry has appeared in *Southern Review*, *Paterson Literary Review*,
Poetry East, *upstreet*, and *Image*.

∿ The Leisure Class

There's nothing demands we hoe
the difficult earth, or grapple with
the stubbornness of weeds, but we can still

be found out in someone else's fields
on a pleasant day, small basket
worn like a bracelet on the forearm

as we bend to pick our own strawberries,
carefully wiping the dust from each
in an individual appreciation

no real farmer could afford,
able to pass by the bruised or beetle-ridden
with no concern for loss, wanting

only the plumpest for our dessert,
to smother in a cream already
whipped, bottled, and set to spray.

Or in winter, with the oil furnace
burning away, we might pass half an hour
splitting wood for the romance of fire,

heft the unfamiliar weight of the axe
over the shoulder, stare at the center
with a tournament archer's eye, and let it fall

toward posed wood, cajole it back out
and strike again until the halves sigh
in parting from each other like a vanquished

doubles team, or we grow tired.
We know crabbing without the persistence
of stinging cuts, knitting the area

of a baby blanket, kneading the dough
for one loaf in the wakeful afternoon.
How amused we are because we write

the term of our indenture,
and know we can always walk out,
as from poor theater.

∾ Odds Are

Before buying in, you slip probability
like a bookmark into a Dickens novel,
flatten with underdog faith the rattiest

bill in your clip, and hand it over
like an ultimatum to the unassuming
fellow who is stacking his fortune

of beer. At the till, you mumble
confirmation of the picks,
and shade in the tiny circles as if

trying to eclipse the repeated emptiness
of a hundred months. Later,
you watch the chaos of whirling

white balls, particles from which
will emerge, on church-organ cue,
the big bang of some lucky one's

luxurious state. For a long moment,
you kneel like a bygone photographer,
blocking out the rest of the world

as you settle the TV's blue veil
over your shoulders and stare
fixedly at the unassembled group.

And then the magnesium blows,
and the captured numbers (not yours)
leave you blinking at the ticket.

You hear behind you the shuffle
of probability, who doesn't feel
betrayed by your trying

to give him the slip, but lays
a heavy hand on your shoulder,
and offers a cup of patience

to console. He knows better
this time than to say out loud
his predictable "told you so."

From the Poet

While not as obvious in its engagement as, say, the Occupy Movement, art,
too, has a role to play in the critical debates about capitalism which feature
in America's most recent period of self-examination. Stepping from the
world's blur and flux into the intimate theater of a lyric poem, the reader
takes a moment to focus on the movement of a thought, to hear its rhythms,
to attend to its seeming digressions, to speculate about the drama which
may have prompted it. In the poems I have contributed to this anthol-
ogy, the drama emerges as a struggle to believe in the egalitarian promise
of our society—to reconcile the possibilities afforded to some by wealth
and the improbabilities that constrain those who do not possess it. The
poems dwell on fantasy and disillusionment: the touristic romance while
day-tripping in another's line of work, the desperate imagining of sudden
deliverance from difficult circumstance. They offer a glimpse of the charm
and consequence of that enduring ideology we call the American dream.
Sometimes the blinders slip and must be faithfully readjusted—or not, if
one is startled deeply enough.

Crystal Williams

A native of Detroit, Michigan, Crystal Williams is the author of four poetry collections, most recently *Detroit as Barn* (Lost Horse Press, 2014). Williams is an associate provost and professor of English at Boston University. She is also an advocate for diversity and equity in the arts and serves on multiple arts and culture boards.

∿ Detroit as Brewster Projects

It must be like this in Iraq,
after a bombing,
the killing. So many
tall, windowless buildings,
mattresses propped
against openings, silence
making the thing
more barbarous.
Danger & death
bloom, balance
in the wind
as if pregnant
heads of weeds.
Always the same
amputee rolling
down the street,
swathed in dark,
fuming garments,
something brutal
about his eyes,
his arms powerful
& veering across the line
set on the street
towards your car
causing you to shift,
swerve. & some other
vacant body standing
on the sidewalk, staring
into the oblong sky.
Another's back turns a corner:
something is happening
out of sight, some life
beneath this life,
in this, these
discarded buildings,
some drug

perching its swart self
against the brink
of light. You can feel
life brimming,
its blistering hand
twisting, its shadowy heart
making a home
in the small, daily changes
of the place: a mattress
two feet to the right,
the tattered cloth hanging
from a third-floor window
when yesterday
it was four floors up.
People perch here,
their bodies a line
you dare not cross.
You do not heed
the STOP sign
waving its angry head.
You speed up when possible,
drive around the entire thing,
the compound
& its recreation center,
the fifteen buildings,
the almost-town houses, parks,
the tennis-turned-basketball
courts, ceded playgrounds,
grass & trees not dead
but not as they are meant to be,
bits of fire & char
edging everything, people,
addicts wandering
their slow way along,
weaving in & out
of the torn & near-gone
chicken fencing as if
their bodies & minds

are fight partners,
legs & backs shuffle & slide,
their red eyes like mortar,
like shells. The city
means to tear it down,
this & what it means.
But today, some man,
the fool, has brought
a clutch of children
to this desert. They are
swinging on the rotted wood
plank of the teeter-totter.
Their mangy Rottweiler
unsteady & tied to a tree.
He watches as the children,
bundled against the cold,
learn to balance & shriek.

∽ At the Water
for A. Van Jordan, from Detroit's RiverWalk

Fifty feet in front of their mother
they lurch towards the dog sitting at your feet,
an eruption of "Yeses!," hands & arms
like new branches twisting skyward.

Their mother calls, "Don't touch that dog!"
& because they are good kids, smart, they heed & halt
three feet from me as she makes her slow way towards us.

All morning I've watched some version of this birthing:
what parents give & cost their children.
But history is nothing more

than a chronic transfer of limitations,
a way of understanding
who we might have been. & who we are

is bodies born of shackles, water.
What these children do in the moment of desire
when the world offers beauty

is an anchor, a shackle forcing them
to yield & gawk at the dark tongue of "no,"
at the foot of a tenacious history circling the edges,

snapping its warnings, making their mother leery
of even a dying, toothless poodle. & so
it's always the white children who claim the dog's body,

their branchy limbs & excited eyes
free of history's shadow.
& Oliver is all possibility:

patient & giving. Here, in the soft fur, in the *Yes*
is where so much, perhaps everything,
is lost.

But then there are two brown children still standing
three feet shy of me, bodies tremorous, humming.
Their mother, her eyes the world's closed doors,

moves past like a storm warning, snips:
"No, I said!
Come on!"

The girl is older, already her hands have rubbed
history's back, her body turns towards the storm.
But the boy's eyes move slowly,

take in every bit of the dog's beautiful mountain, as if
because he understands something about his mother & sister
& self, he must savor, as if he *will* relent to the fact of

his David
& their Goliath—
but he will not bow.

His sister grabs his hand.
Their mother is getting too far away.
Maybe she is seven. He four. Static

for her pull & his tug. But outside of history's reach,
he rallies, moves closer.
"His name is Oliver," I say.

The boy considers me then looks down the RiverWalk,
says quietly to his mother's dark, moving back:
"I want to say 'Hi' to Oliver."

& I am broken with imaginings:
the many corner stops, ways of knowing, cops,
the times this black boy will be forced to call out

his innocence's intention to the world.
&, oh, Lord do I want him to be making himself before me,
place-marking this moment,

deciding against the murky back of history—
the keen-tongued mother, the soft-pull sister—
who he will become. *It can be done*, I think,

but say, "Oliver knows you do, Baby,
& on another day you two will be *great* friends."
He considers me again, nods & then leaves me with

those wide, black orbs, the young, quiet hands, how he grew
small & small, sprinting towards the dark back of history,
calling, "Here I come, here I come!"

From the Poet

When we talk about Detroit, Michigan, in the public sphere, we often talk
about race because Detroit is so dramatically racialized, having housed innu-
merous distinct and self-contained ethnic and racial enclaves. But race in
America is nearly always linked to social class. So the story of Detroit—both
its rise and "demise"—is also the story of social class and mobility.

As a Black girl growing up in the city, being raised by a white mother
complicated my own experience of race. Was I Black? What *was* "Black-
ness"? Was the experience I was having a "Black" experience? Did Black
people have horses and travel and live in Europe, as had I? What was that
haunting moment between me and the summer school kids when, one hot
summer, my mother enlisted me to help her distribute the popsicles she'd

bought for them at the middle school at which she worked? Whence their glare? I was one of them, but was not one of them. And all but my mother knew it.

The above were essentially questions to do with class-based acculturation because physically, as I've stated, I was seen to be and existed as a Black child. And it is often the case that when race is in the room, we don't think to interrogate how social class status is also distinctively at play. So the above questions about race for many years obfuscated a series of deeper and more profound uncertainties to do with class—both literal class status and the ways in which my family, and, to put a finer point on it, my mother, had (and therefore gave me access to) an upper-middle class set of experiences that my friends did not nor would ever have. I was a girl living in one social class circumstance (working class) but acculturated within another (upper middle class). And from this fact emerge many of the more subtle questions in my work as a writer and poet. Such as: In what ways, in what crevices in our collective and individual minds are race and class conflated in this country? And whom does that conflation serve?

These two poems, in different ways, focus on social class. They are written from an outsider's point of view because, due to my social standing and class circumstance, I was an outsider. They are poems that question how class status informs our present—our surroundings, what we believe to be possible for ourselves, what others believe to be possible for us—and our future. They seek to illuminate the ways in which we are complicit in the "othering" of individuals based on social class. And they are written from the lens of a woman who continues to struggle with the shifting terrain of class, race, belongingness, and alienation.

Cate Marvin

Cate Marvin's first book of poems, *World's Tallest Disaster* (Sarabande, 2001), received the 2000 Kathryn A. Morton Prize and the Kate Tufts Discovery Prize. Subsequent books include *Fragment of the Head of a Queen* (Sarabande, 2007) and *Oracle* (W. W. Norton, 2015). Her honors include a Whiting Award and Guggenheim Fellowship. Marvin is a professor of English and creative writing at the College of Staten Island, CUNY.

∿ Stopping for Gas Near Cheat Lake

Trees bent unnatural by wind,
then frozen, looking delicate as jewelry, but unwearable.
Miles of white, palest skin,
and the slash of the road through it. Who named this lake,

who lost? How clear is its water
when not frozen? Do the townspeople refuse to swim in it,
or is it a site for seasonal pleasures?
At the self-serve station, the man insists on filling my tank.

Has everybody in town lost
their money, what can I buy to save them? A cigarette lighter,
a hunter's cap, windshield fluid . . .
Some of my blood's origin is here—a family with white gums

and skin blue as this dusk.
Something not right about it—one year they tested vials
over and over. The doctors:
You'll need to come in again; your blood is strangely thin.

What do you know of your heritage?
The houses are red on Fairchance Lane, their windows look
away from the banks of the lake,
tree-shaded places where lovers embraced. I could stop

the car, stand in those shadows,
and try to find my face on the surface of Cheat Lake.
Or I could walk into town, find
my reflection in the eyes of a distant cousin, lead him

to the water's edge, my white face
haunting him. For those who drowned, for those who escaped,
I demand an answer. Tell me,
tell me where I can find the bastard who named this lake.

∿ Stone Fruit

A train ran   along the track   its pale embankment
by a building with   a hundred   balconies as blue as false

blue eyes are   That was the year I   probably still drunk
the noon after   face a fingerprint pressed   oily surface
I expected great things   You could read all about them
My tongue delivered   a newspaper   onto the grassy slick
of your front lawn   I took out a savings account   I made no friends

I sat in a cafeteria   worrying my face   might lurch
Every breath   clinking into a piggy bank   An important man's
hand   furtive   scurried down my spine while   his secretary
looked away   He cured cancer   I typed it   from dictation
I thought I was   You could read all about it   important
What a long   ago   left my expression scratched on
plexiglass   Slipped a tiny tape into the machine's slot   pressed

a pedal   his voice oozed a letter   I wanted you   a pit to peach
beneath my sheets   to eat   away at the bedding   get to you
at its center   You could read all about it   Like a rodent
rummaging   through the liquor cabinet   Hurt my hands
letter after letter   his voice   a snail   emerging from its shell
I wanted you   you know   enough already   Hands on weekends
extended to perform a jitter on the train   at behest of their delicate

hangover   A hand left   on the train's seat   misplaced
like a mitten   An important man's hand   foraged my neckline
His voice's slug slugging its passage along   my ear's canal
I counted my plots before   they hatched I put all my bombs
in one briefcase   As missions go it   was poorly executed
As far as making   no friends   opening a savings account
I expected great things   That worthless long ago   read all about it

How a lake appeared   its shine a lemon at dusk   a scented coin
passed beneath   the bank teller's   scratched plexiglass   partition
A girl dredged   at its edge   I wanted you like the moon never
wanted to come   in the first place   Had better things to do
would rather   read the paper than peer   before us with its
pocked face   Hands touch   as if just hatched and   stumbling
new into this world   my face in a cafeteria   worrying its features

tending to tics as if   they might be triggered   Blue balconies
empty but for sun-chairs   no body standing   before wintry sun

You will or won't   read about it at all   the train lurching into
the station   where people get off   Saving my account
with words   encoding it as one embroidered   this discreet rose
onto this velvet pillow case   To lean against   to unfold unto
to be important   to be the girl at the lake   make your   nice home

nice   to kiss the important doctor   once he agrees to   cure me
of this   Then to forgo   the moon's dismal features   slap my
body down on your lawn   its entry entire   entreaty   Good-bye
a stick of dynamite tied to its tail   Now omit the girl entry   lake
entry   replace them so   you may view my hands   in our museum
in their new glass case   Nothing is news or new   I wanted to
take the train to you   detonate my face   be your obituary.

From the Poet

"Stopping for Gas Near Cheat Lake" was inspired by a road trip I took
through West Virginia in the late 1990s on my way to visit my maternal
grandmother in western Pennsylvania. I'd discovered a few years prior,
through some routine blood work, that I carried an anemia trait particular
to folks descended from the Mediterranean. But I'd always been told my
family was Scots-Dutch. The only explanation I could think of, then and
now, was that someone in my family, way back, had had an affair with a
Greek or Italian, conceived a child, and managed to keep it a secret.

The poem explores the reality that we might encounter people we are
genetically related to without realizing it. As such, it argues my belief that
no one *really* knows where they come from. But "Stopping for Gas" also
addresses issues of class. What brings the speaker of the poem shame is
that she observes, plainly, how economically challenged this town is; she
assumes because the town is so challenged, there must be Greeks and Ital-
ians there, and therefore questions her destiny: Why, her blood relatives
must live here! Why has she been spared?

Essentially, this poem is a critique of such upper-middle assumptions, of
the liberal mindset regarding charity, and the so-called moral viewpoint with
which enlightened folks pity those sad, ignorant folks in rust-belt regions.
In fact, the speaker *is* a part of this place. It's just that she's been told she
is not. The poem is about poverty, love, and need. And the speaker is trying
to decode the seemingly unrelated events, the infidelity (as indicated by the

name of the lake) that eventually resulted in her existence. Let's just say it's complicated.

"Stone Fruit" is an elegy for myself at the age of 23. You could call it my personal *Bell Jar*.

For a little under a year after graduating college, I moved back home to live with my parents and was employed as a temporary secretary for the National Cancer Institute. That year: 1) I spent no money at all, literally putting every cent I made into a savings account. 2) I frequently raided my parents' amply supplied liquor cabinet to assuage my emotional pain. 3) I was in love with someone who beckoned from far away; we had an agreement that we would, once I'd saved enough money, be reunited. 4) My boss at this job, who was an "Important Doctor," sexually harassed me, and I had no idea whatsoever how to handle this situation, except to avoid him, which was impossible, given that he was my boss.

The poem is about being utterly ripped off. The "important doctor," who should be respectful (and respected!), is grotesque. The True Love turns out to be utterly false, having already traded in his devotion for another girl he has met at a lake. All of this has to do with value. The speaker would not be at the job if she did not need to earn money to move to be with the True Love who has found another. The speaker spends nothing because she so deeply desires to be with the True Love, who no longer writes to her or even thinks of her. The speaker's final impulse is murderous, because the speaker's really been had. She's a girl, after all; she's not worth much.

Kevin Prufer

Kevin Prufer is the author of several collections of poetry,
most recently *How He Loved Them* (2018), *Churches* (2014), and *In a
Beautiful Country* (2011), all from Four Way Books. He's also coeditor of,
among others, *New European Poets* (2008) and *Into English: Poems,
Essays, Commentaries* (2017), both from Graywolf. He is a professor of
English and creative writing at the University of Houston.

∽ The Vast Economies

What is the point of money? said the leopards
at work on the still quivering gazelle.

The gazelle looked at the sky, as if contemplating
the afterlife. Then it closed its eye.

All its verdant afternoons among the foliage
were not even memories anymore. Zero.

What is the point of a salary?
The camera crew, hiding in the tall grass,

recorded the scene. First there was one leopard,
then there were two. When the meat

stopped shuddering, the leopards left,
and three jackals, skulking by the waterhole,

ate next. What is the point of currency?
Zero point. Then came spotted hyenas,

white-backed buzzards, pincered water beetles.
The camera crew sat in the tall grass

eating sandwiches. They'd had a good day's work,
for which they'd be well paid.

The leopards circled them hungrily.
There are, the leopards said, economies

that are greater than those you think you know.
A camera remembers everything

you tell it to remember, but it has no
ideas. Now, it watched the gazelle's bones,

mostly stripped of gore. The gazelle had zero
left to spend. In the dry season,

the sky is always vast and empty. Unnerving. Zero,
zero, zero. And so many leopards

in these hills. The leopards are always hungry.

∾ True Crime

One rich motherfucker bashed another rich motherfucker's face in with a
  gold-plated putter

so the golf club's snack bar was all atwitter

because who knew? Right here at Briar Cliffe Acres?

Good God, said the river.

Good God, said the wind in the pennant, the yacht at the dock. One
  forensic examiner

filled the sand trap with sodium light while another

dusted a nine iron with fingerprint powder.

The half-plastered ladies in tennis whites at the taped-off perimeter

whispered among themselves, *How sad.* And, *Here is a dollar,*

the birds called to each other, pulling grubs from holes in the oak trees.
  Here is a dollar,

a dollar, a dollar.

And one squirrel, burying his nut in the weedy grass by the water hazard,
  muttered,

Got one, then went off in search of another.

And when for a moment the sun disappeared behind a cloud and rain
  watered

the fairway, the Bermuda grass grew greener, thicker and louder

with providence. With God's holy love. Oh rich motherfuckers,

we live in a world of wealth and thunder.

Just ask the rat and his hole full of plunder. Ask the beaver

and his barge of sticks. One of you may be conked beside the golf cart's
  tire, but the other

has two tickets to Zürich, one for himself and one for the dead man's
  daughter.

Such bounty. The sun gilds us until we glitter.

From the Poet

Like any limited-liability corporation, or stock market, or democracy, capital is a kind of fiction that we agree into fact. That is, unlike the house outside my window, with its glowing porch light and hungry cat at the door, capital exists because we all agree about its existence. If, tomorrow, the whole world were to decide that capital did not, in fact, exist . . . then it would vanish from the earth. (We could try all evening to agree the neighbor's cat into nonexistence, and he would probably resent the lack of attention—but, unlike capital, his life would continue.) In this way, money has more to do with, say, religion than it has to do with groceries or cars. Groceries and cars, after all, abide in the world of things. Money, like God, lives in the world of our collective cognition, and behaves that way—hugely and mutably.

It's been argued that what makes us different from animals is not our use of tools (many species of monkeys make and use tools) or language (prairie dogs arguably have words and even a kind of grammar). Rather, what sets us apart is our ability to construct vast fictions and agree those fictions into fact. Our fictional-facts—communism, the legal system, money—are enormously powerful, allowing for the implementation of mind-boggling forces simultaneously and globally.

I like to imagine all of us living beneath a world-covering storm of fictions. They buffet us, setting us in one direction or another, lifting us up or destroying us. Beside us, beneath this storm of fiction, also exists a world of animals and things; they, too, are swept up in the storm, even if they play no part in its creation.

The book I'm writing now is called *The Art of Fiction*, a collection of poems that think about money and politics, wondering about their enormity, intangibility, nonexistence, and effects on the things of the world. I suppose this is most obvious in "The Vast Economies," though it is also the motivating force in the sillier "True Crime." In the first, money is offset by the existence of meat; in the other, it is offset by flesh.

Major Jackson

Major Jackson is the author of five books of poetry,
most recently *The Absurd Man* (W. W. Norton, 2020) and
Roll Deep (W. W. Norton, 2017). He is the editor of Library of
America's *Countee Cullen: Collected Poems* (2013). His honors include
Guggenheim and NEA fellowships, and a Whiting Writers' Award.
Major Jackson is the Richard Dennis Green and Gold University
Distinguished Professor at the University of Vermont and serves
as the poetry editor of *The Harvard Review*.

∿ Selling Out

Off from a double at McDonald's,
no autumnal piñata, no dying leaves
crumbling to bits of colored
paper on the sidewalks only yesterday,
just each breath bursting to explosive fog
in a dead-end alley near Fifth, where on
my knees with my fingers laced behind my head
and a square barrel prodding a temple,
I thought of me in the afterlife.
Only moments ago, Chris Wilder and I
jogged down Girard lost in the promise
of two girls who winked past pitched
lanes of burgers and square chips
of fish, at us, reigning over grills and vats.
Moments ago, a barrage of beepers
and timers smeared the lengths of our chests.
A swarm of hard-hatted dayworkers
coated in white dust, mothers on relief,
the minimum-waged poor from the fast-
food joints lining Broad inched us closer
in a check-cashing line towards the window
of our dreams, all of us anxious to enact
the power of our riches, me in the afterlife.
What did it matter, Chris and I still
in our polyester uniforms caked
with day-old batter, setting out
for an evening of passion marks?
We wore Gazelles, matching sheepskins,
and the ushanka though miles from Leningrad.
Chris said, *Let's cop some blow* despite
my schoolboy jitters. A loose spread
of dealers preserved corners. Then a kid,
large for the chrome Huffy he pedaled,
said he had the white stuff and led us
to an alley fronted by an iron gate on
a gentrified street edging Northern Liberties.

I turned to tell Chris how the night
air dissolved like soil, how jangling
keys made my neck itch, how maybe
this wasn't so good an idea when
the cold opening of gun-barrel
steel poked my head and Chris's eyes
widened like two water spills before
he bounded away to a future of headphones
and release parties. Me? The Afterlife?
Had I ever welcomed back the old
neighborhood? Might a longing
persistent as the seed-corn maggot
tunnel through me? All I know:
a single dog barked his own vapor,
an emptiness echoed through blasted
shells of rowhomes rising above,
and I heard deliverance in the bare
branches fingering a series of powerlines
in silhouette to the moon's hushed
excursion across the battered fields
of our lives that endless night
of ricocheting fear and shame.
No one survives, no one unclasps
his few strands of gold chains
or hums "Amazing Grace" or pours
all his measly bills and coins into the trembling,
free hand of his brother and survives.
No one is forced face down and waits
forty minutes to rise and begin
again his march past the ice-crusted dirt
without friendship or love, who barely knew
why the cry of the earth set him running,
even from the season's string of lights
flashing its pathetic shot at cheer—to arrive
here where the page is blank, an afterlife.

◦ *A Brief Reflection on Torture Near the Library of Congress*

Shouldering a bag of great literature, you glimpse spider silk
extruding from spinnerets, spiraling into
an orb above the restaurant's exit sign. Revenue questions
aside, a diplomat's diamond shirt-studs
sparkle beside Ritzenhoff crystal just when you recall
bike-riding as a child behind a laundry truck,
its bouquets of lavender spraying the road.

Innocuous the lightness of transactions,
exchanging cash, hands touching in meetings.
Some memories are made for the hatchet's blade.
But the Tunisians are rioting today, and a cable station away
above the bar in slow motion, LeBron tosses chalk
into the air like a spell and suddenly you smell
newly opened wads of fresh paper bills.

Yours is the study of steam or how the mind
sprinklers, presently irrigating. Somewhere,
someone is screaming. Where now a military prison,
once a cathedral of trees with signs along the road
that read, "Chute de branches." Waiting for your table,
the bag now feels like a century of offenses.

From the Poet

Just as we are neuropsychologically wired towards some belief in a higher
power, what scientists term the "God spot"—which makes us vulnerable to
all manner of false theology and demagoguery—we are similarly at risk to
the language of advertisement and marketing campaigns, the machinery of
capital, which exploits fundamental fears of loneliness and estrangement.
The alienated woman and man want meaning, long to feel a sense of pur-
pose, to feel connected. This need is a drug. Shopping, participating in the
free market, allows us to feel at one with our neighbors and the world
around us, despite racial and class differences.

Picture the long lines when Apple announces a new product and notice the variety of people waiting to assuage their loneliness. This phenomenon is at the core of capitalism and class ascendancy. The more you have, the more you belong, and the more you are seen by those around you. In our blind buying and selling and our participation in a system that requires exploitation, it is clear that we are harming the planet and our spiritual selves.

Susan Briante

Susan Briante's book *The Market Wonders* (Ahsahta Press, 2016) was a finalist for the National Poetry Series. She is also the author of the poetry collections *Pioneers in the Study of Motion* (2007) and *Utopia Minus* (2011), both from Ahsahta Press. Briante has received grants and awards from *Atlantic Monthly*, the MacDowell Colony, the Academy of American Poets, and the U.S.-Mexico Fund for Culture. She is a professor of creative writing and literature at the University of Arizona. *Defacing the Monument*, Briante's collection of essays on immigration, archives, aesthetics, and the state, was published by Noemi Press in 2020.

∿ from *Mother Is Marxist*

My daughter plays hide and seek with the white floor-length panel curtains in front of a window in our living room. Dusk traffics light, the light scans her. She is gold leafed in the curtain before the window.

Can't you see her gold?

*

"I do not know whether you have seen the building of the Metropolitan Company in New York. . . ," Charles Coolidge Read stated before the Massachusetts Legislature in 1895. "Go up to the directors' room where the floor is soft with velvet carpets and the room is finished in rich red mahogany . . . there you will find these gentlemen who think what a beautiful thing this child insurance is. . . ."

Read insisted that from every block of marble in the Metropolitan Company building peered "the hungry eyes of some starving child."

Advocates said the policies served as funerary insurance as well as protected poor and working-class families against a loss of income at a time when child labor was common. Opponents, like Read, believed it provided incentive for poor or working-class parents to neglect or outright murder their children for profit.

Still, a writer for the *Boston Evening Transcript* declared: "No manly man and no womanly woman should be ready to say that their infants have pecuniary value."

*

The average per student expenditure for public and secondary schools in 2012–2013 ranged from a high in Vermont of $19,752 per student to a low in Arizona of $6,949.

*

The Market scans my child, calculates pecuniary value.

Parents register and respond often seeking out places (the "good" neighborhood or private school) where a child's value is high enough in relation to the needs of others to make them relatively safe

Or a parent may reaffirm existing market valuations.

And if the child is female or presents as female
And if the child is queer or presents as queer
And if the child is poor or presents as poor
And if the child is of color or ethnic or presents as of color or ethnic

A little spark of mica in a field of sand

*

I want to teach my child to shed numbers like a skin in the summer, in the shimmering heat of the ever-warming summer.

*

Mothers attempt to erase the integers, to move decimals, to point out discrepancies in the ledger, disrupt the protocols of exchange.

When the mothers of the victims of police violence march on Washington, DC,

When mothers in Central America set their children like paper lanterns

On a breeze,

When warehouses of children wait at our border,

Mother is Marxist, exposing as false and pernicious the mystification of capitalist instantiations of value, promiscuous relations of value and their violence.

Mother is not a biological or relational subject position, but can be an attitude of resistance before the market.

*

Underfunded public schools show their cinder block, reveal their district paint purchased from the lowest bidder, can't hide their too many desks, their too tired, their underpaid.

You can see it in their lunch trays.

Private schools flaunt their walls of windows, famous architect library, flagstone pathways, full-time counselor.

In such places, children learn to read their market value.

*

A police officer flaunts his gun and in the amount of time your child is afforded to pull their hand from their pocket

You can learn their market value.

*

Unmanned aerial vehicles, better known as drones, scan the Sonoran desert for moving bodies.

There are no accurate numbers for the children killed by U.S. drones outside of our country.

Sometimes when I look up I can see the pale underbelly of the HC-130J Combat King II transport gliding over the streets of my neighborhood or the playground of my daughter's preschool like a hand passing over a velvet rug in the boardroom of an insurance company.

*

If we traveled far enough, we could find 1,000 children waiting on the border, they were walking toward us.

From the Poet

I wrote *The Market Wonders* as a response to the financial crisis of 2008, the endless recession from which many of us have not yet recovered. Literary scholar Lauren Berlant contends that literature can track the everyday effects of the erosion of the social safety net, stagnant wages, and what she terms the fantasies of "upward mobility, job security, political and social equality." With that in mind, *The Market Wonders* became a record of my experiences in the wake of the Great Recession—my act of "limited personal accounting" and an imprint of the dissonance I perceived between how politicians, pundits, and the media described economic events and how the crisis was experienced by the rest of us.

Many of the poems in the book take the stock market as their subject. There are poems in which I personify "the market," poems in which I use the daily closing number of the Dow Jones Industrial Average as a muse, and a poem that runs like a stock ticker along the bottom of the book's pages.

"Mother Is Marxist" is the final piece in the book and the last I wrote. Beyond leveling a critique at corporatism and the market economy as it currently exists in the United States, I wanted to shed light on the way our economic system makes us complicit in a variety of practices that cause the exploitation and oppression of others.

I write these notes on a day when the number of reported U.S. deaths from COVID-19 passes 100,000, and protestors riot in Minneapolis-St. Paul in response to the killing of another black man in police custody. Both in terms of loss of life and loss of livelihoods, the COVID-19 crisis has only exacerbated and underscored what we knew before about the long and devastating trajectory of white supremacy and capitalism. Despite the so-called free market, ethical choices don't always exist in the marketplace. While my credit score follows me like a blessing or curse, our social indebtedness—what we owe each other, what we take from each other—is obscured. In "Mother Is Marxist," I tried to trace some of the social debts I incurred and difficult decisions I faced as a parent. The COVID-19 pandemic has only compounded my sense of indebtedness. I believe that until we understand our social debt, all of our accounts will remain unbalanced.

Sheryl Luna

Sheryl Luna's *Magnificent Errors* received the 2020 Ernest Sandeen
Prize in Poetry from the University of Notre Dame Press. Her book
Seven (3: A Taos Press, 2013) was a finalist for the Colorado Book Award,
and her *Pity the Drowned Horses* (University of Notre Dame Press, 2005)
received the Andres Montoya Poetry Prize. She was recently elected
to the Texas Institute of Letters.

∿ Not One Red Cent

I steal toilet paper,
boil beans and garlic,
bless and baptize pennies.

Kabala: forbearance
in face of insult.

America, I am a connoisseur
of the divided dollar.

For some, a sticky nickel found
comes as joyous as love.

E Pluribus Unum sounds dirty.
Graven image beneath a dirty thumb,

each of my cents declares
someone else's trust in God.

Some say, *God is everywhere*—
even in a copper smelter's lungs.

I count them out on the counter
while the clerk rolls blue eyes,
sets her hand on a fat hip.

She sighs, moves them two by two
into the arc of her palm.

I want to write about whales,
think of Jonah in the belly of one,
punished then expunged onto land.

I walk unlike Jonah,
wool cap pulled over my ears, thinking,
I am not welcome anywhere.

∿ Chico's Tacos

A huge roach skitters along your white stucco
outside wall, streets fill with Impalas, Chevys,

cholos, abuelas. Fathers sit at formica tables;
the tile peels. Counter workers speak Spanish.

Women wear polyester and sandals.
Men don letter jackets from years ago.
The lone striped suit and slick expensive shoes,
always some style. The young in tight jeans,

high heels—nothing like a late-night dance break
at Chico's where caliente red water y dried red chilé-
soaked flautas piled high with cheese, extra cheese,
and indulgence comes like sizzling cola.

The border refinery streams and twin barbed wire
stretches across the river to protect freedom.
It's really cash, and everyone feels it
subliminally in the paper cups.

* * *

The Indio-beggar, baby hanging off her slanted back,
an old styrofoam cup held out, eyes dusk.
In the past there were droves, Juáreñas, aliens,

now scattered like tumbleweeds across the desert.
The flame at Asarco once ablaze, now snuffed.
Copper smelting killed the land; children can't play
in the sand. Languages mix—

There will be no celebrities, no Lexus,
no thin models, maybe Oscar de la Hoya, mariachis,
the musical song of a city drowning
on the edge of nowhere.

* * *

You won't find a beach.
Some days sand blows hair hard and skin feels
pecked by a chicken in the valley, near Ysleta,
where the Tigua Indian Casino closed
after East Texas oil men lost their wealth.
Underground water near Hueco Tanks bartered

like people's lives—but you can always find
Chico's tacos being devoured. A small pleasure
for the poor, and those who grow rich return to
Chico's because it's something of home,
something to be found nowhere else.

And why would anyone care—
it's no bluegrass bar, it's no rock-n-roll café—
no, it's slimy, crowded, sweaty. It's full of Mexicans,
a few gringos, y viejitas. Great U.S.A., patriotic home,
this is your hidden pleasure domain.

Maquiladora workers in Juárez murdered,
Mexican-Americans hating Mexicans, cumbias,
rancheras, dollar dances, quinceañeras, gay bars,
maricones dance in the streets of Juárez.
Scenic drive overlooks a million lights.

* * *

There is no full circle back for some.
It's all dry joblessness. Chico's, Lucky's,
and always the wretched university
with its Bhutanese architecture
large and looming on the smoggy border
like some paradoxical crime.

~ The Loser

Although I lost the car, the house, the better job,
my eyes wander everywhere and nowhere.

I'll dive deep into the water, splash
my animal hair. My torso sunned
and bare. I'll grow strawberries and melons,

and my vegetables will bloom dark green.
I'll dream and un-dream a million old things,
own a gazebo, a stone bridge, a palomino.

My imaginary cottage will have birdsong
and shade. The sun will purchase my gaze.
I'll count heaven in my forgotten language.

Weary of salesmen who want me to sell time,
I wander lush-lazy to and fro, sing
while trees are taken by light.

Hustlers wear their shoes shined. I am barefoot
in the stream. They left us behind
among daffodils floating in the light.
Crabapple blossoms ebb white with sky.

From the Poet

I recently read an essay in which a poet wrote that poetry has become all about the money. He mentioned the large cash prizes and the fact that many poets teach in higher education. He concluded that poetry has become a cushy way to support yourself. I wanted to tell him my own journey towards living on a limited budget. I suspect my path is no different than that of many other poets who struggle financially.

I grew up on the southern border in El Paso, Texas, where few people have money but seem for the most part happy. My poem "Chico's Tacos" is about this bicultural and bilingual city. Early on, I saw the poverty across the border in Mexico. People lived in cardboard houses, and many begged on the Cordova Bridge. I once saw a man with no legs propelling himself with his palms and arms down the street. I never forgot these stark images of poverty.

I earned a doctorate based on a professor's assurance that the job market for English professors would blossom. She said many professors who had earned their PhD's on the post-WWII GI Bill would be retiring in the late nineties. It never happened. I earned the doctorate but found myself living on the equivalent of minimum wage as an adjunct instructor with no health insurance. Also, I had a large student-loan debt.

I struggled, unaware than I had post-traumatic stress. This fact, coupled with not having much money and no familial help, left me vulnerable and afraid. Things got so bad that I was losing student assignments, gradebooks, and found it almost impossible to read through students' papers. There were summers I literally praised finding change in my couch's crevices. I soon realized I could no longer teach as an adjunct.

Poetry helped me survive emotionally. The poems included in this anthology are based on that journey.

I applied for Social Security disability in December of 2010. I started receiving payments in February of 2012. I also received Section 8 housing from the county and eventually had my student loans discharged. For the first time in my life, I had a steady income and affordable housing. Now I am doing better than ever financially. I am still poor, but I feel blessed and unashamed. I am a survivor.

Eric Gansworth

Eric Gansworth, S·ha-weñ na-sae², is an enrolled Onondaga
writer and visual artist, raised at the Tuscarora Nation. He is a
professor and the Lowery Writer-in-Residence at Canisius College.
His books include *If I Ever Get Out of Here* (Arthur A. Levine Books,
2013), winner of the YALSA Best Fiction for Young Adults, *Extra Indians*
(Milkweed Editions, 2010), and *A Half-Life of Cardio-Pulmonary Function*
(University of Syracuse Press, 2008). His most recent book is
Apple (Skin to the Core) (Levine Querido, 2020).

∿ A Half-Life of Cardio-Pulmonary Function

I used to think
that if I loved hard
enough and long enough
passion would always win out

like the way I loved
cologne, venturing teenaged into
congested malls, abusing testers
only a salesperson surly enough

inquiring if he or she could help
me in any way, spitting
the prices of even the smallest
bottles of the scents I had

slathered on, forcing me out
in a cloud of confidence
that I was the Calvin Klein
Man, not the Old Spice

Man, not the Zest
Man, and certainly not
the My Drafty House is Warmed Badly
by Kerosene Heaters Man

impervious to my real
life where I would sneak
down in the middle
of the night, passing

snow collecting
on the inside of the window
sill, trying to descend
the stairs silently

to complete the night lying
before the stove's vents blowing
sooty warm air deep into my
sleeping lungs, clutching

a broken lacrosse stick
to intimidate rats so brazen
our housecats accepted
them as equal occupants

until I exit those automatic
doors, leave fountains where
just out of range I envy white
families tossing entire

cigarettes packs' worth
of what they call spare
change, wishing for things
they could already buy if they wanted

laughing as those presidential
faces fall sometimes up
and sometimes down, all drowning
in three inches of chlorinated well water

return to the reservation
where my sister-
in-law embraces me later
the same day, drawing

deeply, saying she loves
the scent of burned heating
oil on men, that it reminds
her of when she and my brother

dated and she would hold
him long in those last moments
before allowing him to walk out
her door, meander through snowy

grooves, finding his way home
while she looked out windows
where ice crystals gathered
on the proper side of the pane

holding her breath as long as she
dared, letting his presence seep
out only when she could no longer
bear, leaving him to be a vapor ghost

on her window, a fog sure
to vanish even before she turned
from the window and here I am
years later, living in that same

state, you miles away and I,
knowing how presence disperses
into air, wonder how long
I can hold my breath.

∼ Wade Wakes Me with Sweat, Tears, and, Yes, the Rest Too

We've worked together through high
school as undesirable labor
at a county garage doing the chores
most hated by those employees pulling in
a retirement, health benefits, vacation,
and more than minimum wage, but it is
a job where I can make more money
per week than my family lives on
and I have new clothes for the first time
in my life, and even a leather jacket
on layaway for when the winter rolls around
and in that time I have learned
from the laborers how to
hold my breath while hosing vomit
from a school bus floor, how to
apply for workman's compensation
when I trip in the upstairs
storage area, detonate a fluorescent
tube, rain down a halo of gas, glass, and dust
all around myself, how to
wipe piss and greasy pubic hair

from the floor before the urinal
with a wet paper towel and boot toe, how to
conjure important work from thin air
when a supervisor arrives, how to
unplug a toilet clogged
with used sanitary napkins and loudly confront
a room full of aging women in order
to avoid that exact situation
a second time, and every second week
two hundred dollars finds its way
into my empty pocket, and this is
the good life until one day, I leave
the men's room window open wide
to air it out where Wade walks head first
into its corner, and as blood spurts through
his flattened fingers from his forehead
like the children of some Greek
God whose name I have forgotten
tainting the white porcelain of my freshly Cometized
sink and I tell him to bleed somewhere else
and as it runs down his face, into his eye
he asks me if this is what I want
for the rest of my life, an accumulation
of scars collected from people leaving doors
almost open for me, and in my silent rinsing
he tells me quietly to apply for college
and this is truly the first time anyone
has ever made this particular request.

From the Poet: Not Meant for This

I was born and raised at Tuscarora Nation. After the reservation elementary school, Tuscarora children went to a regional high school of 1,500 "academically tracked" students, largely white middle class. Those placed in the top and middle curriculum tracks expected to attend colleges of their choice. Those in the lower tracks were encouraged to explore vocational classes. Initially, I'd been placed in the high group, but after a brief issue in middle school, I was reassigned into the lowest sections.

I imagine the guidance counselors concluded my initial ranking had been too generous. Students living below the poverty line rarely made it into the academic achiever track, and we were visible to all. We were eligible for labor jobs at the school and a free lunch. Every day, we lined up to receive our meal cards at the front of the cafeteria, and our peers, from their extracurricular club rooms, often saw us cleaning the school. From middle school through graduation, I stood in the lunch ticket line, and worked at the school's garage, to ease my family's household bills.

When the time came, I asked my guidance counselor if the SAT fee could be paid in installments. He said some people weren't meant for college, and that my labor job was giving me excellent training for the job market. I accepted that, without taking the SAT, I had no chance at higher education. By September, most of my friends had left for college or the military. I worked in a scrapyard, sorting through machinery for valuable metals, mostly copper.

That November, I was desperate to get out of the cold, and I attended an open house for the local community college. It had an open-door policy, with no SAT requirement, encouraging applicants without traditional credentials. I began to develop my mature voice as a writer and painter in that college. I'd been writing and painting on my own since the fourth grade, but my place in the economic food chain did not allow for those interests to be taken seriously in my high school.

Those early economic realities have shaped the thematic lens of my work. I have few regrets, especially considering the number of people I know who gave up on artistic lives. Still, how might things have been different if my high school's officials hadn't regularly equated financial class with intellectual potential? How many others listen when they are told they're not meant for academic opportunities because of their family's economic legacy?

Devon Balwit

Devon Balwit's collections include *We Are Procession, Seismograph* (Nixes Mate Books, 2017) and *Motes at Play in the Halls of Light* (Kelsay Books, 2017). Her poems can be found in *Cincinnati Review, Carolina Quarterly, Fifth Wednesday, Aeolian Harp Folio*, and *Red Earth Review*, among others. She teaches in Portland, Oregon.

∽ *Un-American*

"Here's a dollar bill and some change in this waste basket. . . . How
did you make that mistake?"

"It was left over," he said. "I didn't need it."

—Flannery O'Connor, *Wise Blood*

The thought that someone might be indifferent to it steams us
like sitting next to a teetotaler at a bar when we're tying
one on. How can you not want to plunge your head into the
champagne fountain, then make yourself puke to clear space
for more? To refuse is un-American. Your lack of attachment
grinds the assembly line to a halt, leaves dad slumped in his
recliner while mom pulls double shifts washing invalids. It's
like having two hearts with those on the transplant list dying
for one. Take your monkish indifference elsewhere, dig a den
with the foxes. The rest of us raise greyhound heads at dawn
and get running, lapping the track after the mechanical rabbit.
We prick ears to the silent whistle, salivate, and whine. I
wouldn't want to be you—the only dog out of harness—while
the laden sled thunders behind. You don't earn, you don't eat.

∽ *Minding the Gap*

We went to the same private school, each year the cost of college,
yet sharing a classroom isn't the same as sharing a class, stepping
off mass transit and walking half a block to the door not the same
as gunning a sweet-sixteen cherry red convertible, smashing it, and
driving the identical one a day later, the burp of Tupperware not
the polite cough of a personal assistant sent to deliver the sushi you
ordered, the four-day vacations at grandma's beach house we thought
so spiffy, not quite surfing in Rica or hanging in Biarritz, our brand-
name clothing lifted from the school lost and found. And then, when
the universities that accepted us covered "all but" thirty thousand
a year, doors that opened for you slammed for us, the bottom line
being we can share a page in your yearbook, but we won't work
together, won't live in similar houses, won't summer on the same
shore, won't wear the same brands, eat the same food, drop the same

names. What we studied wasn't as important as what we knew without being taught—that who we become is decided before we ever open a book. From our first wail, some of us are given more space and cleaner air, will fly more miles, leave a bigger footprint. Some of us will stumble, but never be allowed to hit the ground. Braces alone aren't enough for a million-dollar smile. I can stand tall but still not be tall enough not to be looked down on. This is what I learned at our alma mater. This is what I still know.

∾ invocation

lucre, my love	my dear one, my darling
three-headed Cerberus	between me and misfortune
clang your portcullis	rattle your armor
scare away creditors	be doughty with debtors
fatten my billfold	vault away bitcoin
I twirl in my pasties	a pole dance for Croesus
a slut in my writing	a hoi polloi harlot
come to me, come to me	spill upon altars
a day job, a night job	a blow job, a snow job
a raise, a rout	a riot, a handout
anything helps	says my sign on the freeway
pick up all pennies	dig beneath cushions
visit the grannies	keep up with the aunties
lucre, my love	my dear one, my darling

From the Poet

Some of my parents' most spectacular fights were about money. Just as, at university, some of the most awkward lies I heard were spoken by my wealthier classmates trying to obscure their class status. These verbal dances continue as my adult peers try to minimize the potential awkwardness of our class differences. As a poet and teacher, I've long realized that talent, dedication, and cashflow do not correlate. As a parent, I see how money translates into privilege, providing children with education, travel, orthodontics, and connections. Now that I'm aging, I fear that, in the coming decades, my lack of wealth will mean limitation, isolation, and even physical suffering. When my children confess they want to make different career decisions than I have, I understand.

The current pandemic-related crisis has seen two job losses in our family—that of my husband and my daughter. Transferring my husband to my work health insurance plan means that one-third of my income goes to paying for that insurance since my boss picks up only a small portion of the premium for our family of five, surely not a great way to save up for our golden years. Our retirement savings themselves are going to support our three college-attending children in a time when employment and re-employment prospects look bleak. Writing, at least, reflects one unquench-able source of (inner) wealth.

I don't know that poetry can directly impact the huge economic inequal-ities of the U.S. But at least the process of crafting and reading poems can allow the sufferer the illusion of control—and the chance to spend a little time in good company.

Denise Duhamel

Denise Duhamel's most recent books of poetry are
Second Story (University of Pittsburgh Press, 2021) and *Scald*
(University of Pittsburgh Press, 2017). *Blowout* (University of Pittsburgh
Press, 2013) was a finalist for the National Book Critics Circle Award.
Among her other titles are *Ka-Ching!* (University of Pittsburgh Press, 2009)
and *Queen for a Day: Selected and New Poems* (University of Pittsburgh
Press, 2001). A recipient of fellowships from the Guggenheim Foundation
and the National Endowment for the Arts, Duhamel is a professor at
Florida International University in Miami.

∾ $100,000

As a kid I loved being the banker in Monopoly, in The Game of Life—the
pink and yellow bills not quite as big as our U.S. currency, but closer to
food stamps. The board games had no coins, snubbing the paltry dimes of
hobos and kids. I had a penny collection, round slots in a blue cardboard
folder, and I'd search for dates while rummaging through my parents'
change, hunting for pennies that became worth more than pennies, the
value of what is rare. The 1943 copper-alloy penny, the 1955 penny with
the year stamped twice, the 1924 penny with the letter "S" after the date.
I loved rolling coins in wrappers, my favorite being the quarters, with
their hefty $10 payoff; my least favorite the nickels, the same amount of
trouble for only $2, even though I kept a lookout for one of those rare
1913–1938 buffalos. My grandmother gave me a porcelain bank, not a
piggy but a cat, and I filled it within a year, not realizing there was no hole
with a rubber stopper on the bottom, no way to get the money out. There
are still coins in the bottom of that cat! I tried my best to slip them out
with a knife through the slot in the kitty's head, but even after several days
at the kitchen table, I couldn't retrieve a few fifty-cent pieces, though I
remembered their clinkety-clank going in. There is a metaphor here
somewhere, that making money can be messy and aggressive, that wimps
like me will never truly take a hammer to a gift. I was a teenager by the
time the bicentennial quarters went into circulation, a Revolutionary
drummer on the back instead of an eagle. They were too plentiful to
warrant collecting—or maybe I was just too busy working as a
supermarket cashier after school, making sure all the heads on my bills
were facing the same way. I'd open a roll of coins by banging them on the
tray in my drawer, without a thought to the children's ghost fingers
stacking them, learning to count. Now I'm too busy to roll. I recently
dumped a plastic bag full of change in a coin changer in the supermarket,
and even after the machine's commission, got $70. I am richer than I ever
imagined I'd be. I've held lira, pesetas, pounds in my hand, and now the
Euro—peach, aqua, embellished with silver stripes; the smallest bill a 5,
all the rest coins. As a teenager I loved being the banker in Monopoly, in
The Game of Life, the pink and yellow bills vaguely what I thought of as
sophisticated, European.

∾ $400,000

My uncle was a big mucky-muck in a supermarket chain. He liked
throwing lavish get-togethers with all the complimentary liquor he'd
received from buyers. He was the first to serve Pringles, Orville
Redenbacher's Gourmet Popcorn, Mrs. Field's Cookies, Starburst Fruit
Chews, Reese's Pieces, and Miller Lite—all free samples, he explained.
He started voting Republican when he got rich, which led to all kinds of
fiery arguments at the Christmas parties he'd host. My uncle had a silver
tree decorated with blue glass balls, which seemed the height of luxury to
me and a snub to our traditional green one, our folksy homemade
ornaments. But even though he drove a Cadillac now, he was loyal to his
family, getting his nieces and nephews union jobs at the market as soon
as we were sixteen. My high school friends who worked at factories and
gas stations marveled at my cushy situation, my yearly raises, the time
card I punched—even if I worked only eight minutes extra, the
supermarket had to pay me for a full quarter of an hour. I was required to
wear a horrid red smock and chirp, "Have a nice day," the company's
slogan, at the end of each transaction. The break room was filthy and the
manager, a lech. But even so, I knew I had it pretty good. My uncle looked
a little like Richard Nixon, whom he defended until the end—*Everyone will
remember China, not Watergate,* he said. My uncle's other idol was Frank
Perdue with whom he'd had a breakfast meeting once in a Dunkin'
Donuts in Boston. He told this story over and over, as though Frank
Perdue was as talented as Frank Sinatra. *A hell of a man,* my uncle cooed.
A visionary! Frank wanted more room for his chickens in the meat case,
more Perdue signs. He insisted that the supermarket brand "price
comparison" posters be removed. My uncle was Nixon, and Perdue was
China. Or maybe it was the other way around. The negotiations were
fierce and went on for hours, the waitresses refilling their coffee cups
actually changing shifts. Both my uncle and Frank were on diets but,
needing more energy to persevere, decided to split a maple frosted with
sprinkles. When the check came, my uncle tried to pick it up. *No,* Frank
said. *I don't want any special favors. Let's go Dutch.* The bill came to $1.33
and Frank Perdue—this is why he was rich, my uncle alleged—debated
who should leave that extra penny.

∾ $600,000

In 1986, my roommate talked me into getting my first ATM card. We
both had a checking account at Citibank, which became known as
Shitibank because it wouldn't divest its South African assets. I stood in a
long line with other New Yorkers—but when it was my turn, the sun
shone on the screen so I couldn't quite see it. I squinted, took off my
sunglasses, then put them back on. My PIN didn't work—maybe I was
doing something wrong? I tried my code again, along with several
variations, until the machine swallowed my card. For one of her gallery
shows, Sophie Calle photographed people through the security cameras
at Paris ATMs. The baffled, the frustrated, the blasé, the elated dad with
his toddler on his shoulders. I was inspired to do a spin-off project about
PIN numbers—not simple birthday codes, but the codes of obsessions:
bingo2, leather88, Whitman13. Of course, my project stayed pre-
conceptual. Who would tell me their passwords? Even if I convinced them
that I was an honest person, that more than one time in the early days of
ATMs I'd walked up to a machine that read *Can I help you with anything
else?* because a customer had left too soon. A few times I pressed "yes,"
but only to check a stranger's checking account balance—I never
attempted to withdraw even $20. At some point, my roommate started
being late with her rent, which terrified me, as my name was the only
name on the lease. She started borrowing my sweaters and stuffing them,
smelling like smoke, back in my drawer. She'd come into my room in the
middle of the night, crying about the abortion—she still owed me for that,
too. She'd lost her job as a receptionist because two lines rang at once, and
she just shut off the ringer. When she was three months behind, I told her
she'd have to leave. She said I'd go far in this world because I was a
conscienceless bitch, even though I'd changed from Shitibank to
Chemical. When she moved out, she took everything we'd bought
together—ice cube trays, the shower curtain, a throw rug, a teakettle.
When I dusted and mopped her empty room, I found a red mesh bag
filled with candy coins covered in gold foil—the chocolate was cheap, a bit
waxy, but the foil was sturdy—and when I was careful enough, I could
pull off one of the serrated paper sides without ripping it and hold what
looked like a gold bottle cap in my palm.

From the Poet

The first section of my book *Ka-Ching!* is called "play money," containing ten prose poems I wrote to actually fit on the back of $100,000 play money bills I found at a thrift store. I experimented by putting the play money in my printer—play money is blank on the back—until I made ten poems that were all the same size. So I wrote one million dollars worth of poems!

Money is quite a taboo subject in the arts, as well as in polite company. I have always been interested in breaking taboos in my work—speaking the unspeakable, saying the unsayable—and have written a lot about sex and gender. I guess money was the logical (or illogical) next step. In the early 2000s, money was in the zeitgeist. Television personalities like Suze Orman and Jim Cramer became pop culture figures. I must have picked up on that. *Ka-Ching!* came out shortly after the financial crash of 2008.

So much of what is important in life cannot be measured by a dollar amount. It seems unnecessary to state that, but sometimes I have to state it to remember that it's true.

Kathleen Winter

Kathleen Winter is the author of three poetry collections:
Transformer (The Word Works, 2020), *I will not kick my friends*
(Elixir Press, 2018), and *Nostalgia for the Criminal Past* (Elixir Press,
2012). She has received fellowships from the Sewanee Writers' Conference,
Texas Institute of Letters, the Dora Maar House, James Merrill House,
Vermont Studio Center, and Cill Rialaig Project. She teaches creative
writing at Sonoma State University and Santa Rosa Junior College.

∾ Country Club Fourth of July

Mother is out of breath with it—
the studded gladiator sandal—

the newsprint ad for it
which thrills her cloistered heart

and strains the worked-up muscles
of her chest.

American crawl, propel me,
small and hungry, gripping

a plastic bag,
toward the bounty of illusion

water magnifies:
thousands of goldfish and coins

tossed in the luminous
chemical pool.

∾ The Grammar of Ornament

We shed slickers at the entrance,
    before woodcuts of peasants,
bare-breasted. In a downstairs hall
    Rome's muscle glows on the torsos.

Tonight adults will dream about sex
    and the children about ice cream.
Take a right at the sarcophagus:
    carnivorous 18th Century,

your still life of rabbit and pheasant
    is titled *The Pâté.*
The museum freed a grand chandelier
    from a duchess:

rock crystal fissures
    glimmer in electric light

but imagine with candles!
   You're a servant flaming dishes

and wicks, soot snowing dusk
   upon London. This saint's feet
are painted to extremes:
   each toe has its own personality.

Between twin arcs of staircase
   aluminum Eros streaks,
on leave from Piccadilly.
   He flings a leg back toward empire,

balances his washboard
   core over an ankle.
Outside gilded frames,
   typed cards remark dates

and makers, buying habits
   of the British middle class.
Ornaments of grapevine
   and orb, peacock feather fan,

sterling teapot shaped
   like an udder—what middle class
could afford this grammar,
   the mummy's self-satisfied smile?

∾ Hipster Squid

High & dry, at five o'clock the light leaches
out around me, knotted & waiting to be bought,
boxed, gifted. Mounted on a laminate plaque,
I live in Oak Cliff in a curated shop on a short
street where whole pies go for a day's wages.
In the thick of former barrio, four blocks
of boutiques, bars, dry-clean-only T-shirts.
Three of the old hood's vice squad loiter
on a corner, wishing for a grifter come to lift
December's music from the streetlight trees.

How am I ever getting out of here? Who has
the scratch for a hand-knitted squid?

From the Poet

The tone is quite different in each of my poems included here, but they
share an adjunct professor's suspicious (and yes, jealous) attitude toward
people with a level of wealth that lets them forget about money. The closer
to broke I happen to be, the more precisely I know how much I have in the
bank, how much I spent on lunch yesterday, and how many days will pass
until payday. People who aren't fiscally challenged can go for months of
living and spending with only a blurry idea of how much they can draw
on—they just know it's plenty.

The idea of waste also comes into play in these poems, whether it's the
inflated price of a pair of designer shoes advertised in the *New York Times*,
or the expensive burials of ancient Egyptian elites, or a thirty-five-dollar
cherry pie in a Dallas boutique bakery. Issues of class and cash fascinated
me as an undergraduate taking Marxian philosophy courses at the Uni-
versity of Texas, and still intrigue and appall me. Our nation faces both
extreme and increasing income inequality, and the toxic impacts of uncon-
trolled, anonymous campaign contributions exacerbated by the Supreme
Court's misguided *Citizens United* judgment. Income disparities are even
more critical now, when COVID-19 has affected poor communities in the
U.S. much more drastically than wealthy ones. Paying attention to money
issues will always be important to me as a poet, voter, and taxpayer.

Jane Mead

Jane Mead was the author of five collections of poetry, most recently *World of Made and Unmade* (Alice James Books, 2016), which was nominated for a National Book Award. She was the recipient of a Guggenheim Foundation Fellowship, a Whiting Award, and a Lannan Foundation Completion Grant. For many years, she worked as Poet-in-Residence at Wake Forest University and managed her family's ranch in northern California. Mead died in September 2019.

∾ Money

Someone had the idea of getting more water
released beneath the Don Pedro Dam
into the once-green Tuolumne,—

so the minnows could have some wiggle room,
so the salmon could lunge far enough up
to spawn, so that there would be more salmon

in the more water below the dam.
But it wasn't possible—by then the water
didn't belong to the salmon anymore, by then

the water didn't even belong to the river.
The water didn't belong to the water.

∾ from *Cove*

**

I'm no lover of human skin in any shade.
I prefer the animals who live
without their souls—how there's nothing

that floats away on a sea of sky
like a what-did-you-say-we-were by and by.
Hell, I don't even know what I am

right now,—a forgettable fact?
I don't know a thing, but I like
to hope I'll get this figuring figured—

that God will lean out of some cloud
bellowing my name, waving my ribbon.
Oh hell. Have mercy on us—

someone. Anyone. Anyone who is watching.
Save up. Save us. (Big job.)

****

I was raised on the enlightened consumerism
of upper bohemia, fell from grace into
lower bohemia—which is defined by

an inability to take adult responsibility:
don't sell me anything on credit.
In fact, don't sell me anything at all.

Thank you. Now listen here—
I took the workshop on basic functioning,
studied the universal precautions

and the diagram of the evacuation plan,
I sent away for the free booklet
on why I was born. You can trust me

with your children now—the eggs
are hidden in the bushes to signify
rebirth, bread in the ovens, beans

on the stove, knife in the drawer.
To signify rebirth.

* * * * *

I came out of the dark hills
and the dark hills own me. I have
no patience for the sticky-minded

stratums. The concern of the comfortable
for the comfortable makes me sick. Meanwhile,
the red leaves spin on their axes of air,

different leaves now, different axes,
same big death. And wouldn't we love
to shrug now and just say sorry?

Apparently not say sorry.
Let's not talk about it.
I wish I lived in an opium cloud.

* * * * * *

Listen—it's all the same:
the world in the needle,
the iron in the iron-colored sky.

There's a cove in every leaf.
Don't ask me how it got there
but it's like our love for thin air,

the distraction of the kiss, our hope
for something beyond what we can
plainly see—the poisoned planet poisoning.

Kmart may just well be as successful
an organization as we're up to.
But if I could tell you how to live

chances are I'd get drunk instead
and turn into some kind of stand-up
comic, say look!—the rust is unfurling

as far as the human eye can see!

From the Poet

In my poem "Money," the tension between the title and the body of the
poem is meant to reflect the ultimate absurdity and self-destruction inher-
ent in the forces of a free market economy—the whirlwind of commerce
that wants to catch up everything in its path. A river might survive by being
protected from the consequences of these forces, i.e., by being removed
from the marketplace. Or a river might survive by being given a legal way
to participate in the fray, that is, by becoming a stakeholder—represented
by environmental groups—in the water it carries, just as municipalities
and agriculture make their claims. Absent this representation within a
legal framework, we are led to the absurdity of a river shrinking and warm-
ing and failing to support its fish populations because . . . the water doesn't
"belong to" the river. The poem takes this absurdity one step further: "The
water didn't belong to the water."

In "Cove," the speaker is crazed with grief and despair at the "poisoned
planet" to such a degree that she begins to lose her connection to the people

around her and to her humanity. Her belief that Kmart "may just well be as successful an organization as we're up to" and that she can't be trusted to buy on credit—that is, to participate in the system—raises the question of how one can keep one's sanity within a basically insane context.

My life has been an attempt to negotiate these forces and balances—to keep body and soul integrated despite their competing demands.

Allison Hedge Coke

Allison Hedge Coke has published six books of poetry, a memoir, and a play. The 2020 Dan and Maggie Inouye Distinguished Chair in Democratic Ideals at the University of Hawai'i at Manoa, Hedge Coke's awards include a Fulbright, the First Jade Nurtured SiHui Female Excellent Foreign Poet (China), an American Book Award, a King-Chavez-Parks Award, an IPPY Medal, a PEN Southwest Book Award, and a Lifetime Achievement Award from NWCA. A former sharecropper and fisher, she is a distinguished professor at the University of California, Riverside.

∾ *Off-Season*
for fieldworkers and framers like me

Early, on grayest morning, when we
nettled deep in between rows,
tobacco and sweet potato,
both two seasons away from planting,
you reasoned I belonged there,
flowing like creek water
below our bright leaf fields,
then showing only golden stubble and root.
You said I'd never make it
swinging hammers and teething
saws of Inland Construction.
I raised my back wings, those muscles
wrought from priming rows, muscles
which cradled my ribs and sides. I
chucked tools in the flatbed, headed
north, to the city sprawled out like
scattered masonry and split rails, Raleigh,
smoked factory winds and speakeasy halls.

A white chicken fell off a Tyson rig,
just a bit ahead of me on Saunders Street.
I called her "Hooker"
from walking down the red-light street.
The Inland guy hiring was big and red,
sat behind a door laid flat for a desk on cinder block.
He chuckled much like you
at the sight of me, but the fields and breaking horses
justified my ninety pounds of lean.
Next day he had me start out on a crew full of men.
Men who'd never seen a woman work
that way in town, first
time I had a chance to operate a backhoe,
first time I got to frame, and when I swung the hammer
full leverage, three pounds drove in sixteen-pennys straight.
In six weeks, I made foreman.
Just before I drove back to you.

"Hooker" almost got pecked to death
by our bantams—citified as she was.

I laid out so much money, I beat
what you pulled in for fall. We settled in
for the long freeze. You ate ridicule and haste.
We were never the same,
until spring when the fields reclaimed
us as their own and we returned
to what we both knew and belonged to.
The off-season only an off-shoot
in what we were meant to be.
You never did know this part
of who I am. Fieldworker, or framer,
I only showed you what you said I couldn't be.

∽ This He Learned by Being American
    for Walter

He called me a "welfare slut" and
I never spoke to him again.

This he learned by being American
        by trying to be white.

I hung up the phone,
diapered my youngest,
and got ready for school and work.

The food stamps burned my fingers
in Safeway on the way home.
That night felt especially heavy
wondering where the harlot lay.

I questioned my abstinence
as if a name pushed on me
would materialize into something promiscuous.

I questioned my worth.

This he learned by being American.

∽ Wealth

When it was over

everything dust   blown
chickens, ducks, horses, plows
Model A, Mark III

       Dad still keeps the key
mounted to this tin shed wall.

Dust, then,
         everything blown.

Dust, dust, dust.

Still they came around
asking for whatever he held
          to feed,
eleven of them he carried
and the others,   dozens.

Grandpa the generous
gave his last rhyme
in riddle rhythms
without capital consensus.

"I thought you were rich."
They said.

As Granddad and his family
walked away from this
repossessed dugout,
chunk of ground,
earthen home,

flushed and empty,
chin up, Cherokee . . .

"Am, my family's alive."
He affirmed, shaking his head loose
from assumption
he had anything left to give.

As if he'd ever been fund wealthy
longer than a week.

Still Granny fed them
before they walked on.

He insisted. She couldn't imagine
               any other way.
It was their manner. Their spark.

Once, his land had put out,
he gave way 'cause others called,
split between closer relatives
who camped all alongside throughout.

Until it was done.

Back to corn, squash, beans, tomatoes.
Back to working for railroads,
farmers, farriers, friends, foes.

Back to the shoulder plow,
another hold, far from rooted homes,
rotted worlds behind them,
then the dust,

               dust,   dust,   dust.

Still, in this world,
down generations now.
Others come wanting
          something
                    they're sure we have.

We pull out our checkbooks, cards,
overdraw ourselves.

Feed them.

From the Poet: Halves

Capital is conflict. Capital is *means* versus *meaningful*, is competition and detrimental results to anyone without.

Capital is criminal to the sustenance of the planet—if/when the means is without generosity and the equalizing grace of gifting. The core resourced, and to the wealthiest, the spoils. To the impoverished, no matter how little they have, someone will come with need or claim until they have no more. Money follows money. Its property is charismatic and relies on the labor and despair of others to fuel its pathway beyond the reach of those who need most.

Money sits at a table of the monied and gains favor by reflecting desire not truth.

Truth is, some people never stand straight after stoop-labor in childhood. Some never right after falls from the saddle. A piece of some never leaves tobacco fields. Some never leave repetitive motion, the rigid musicality in labor. Some forever by water awaiting the brimming pop of surface to pluck fish, while the monied pluck human lives as if for their own source meal.

Our hearts are not made of capital. We are reciprocal beings. Our brains nourished best by simplicity, by peace.

Some will remain unbroken by "betters'" constant scold. Some still cope when death calls. Some never could.

Comfort is subjective. When bedding on the ground is routine, the ease of curling without cramp gives a bit of solace to sleep. A child sleeping winter nights in laundromat dryers, for remaining heat there, or against a concrete bank under a trestle or overpass, knows nothing of a bed cradling the body without effort. The only constant—unpredictable in every venue— is the dreamscape.

Hunger is subjective, too. To some, six months passed without chewing, gums half-receded from malnutrition, hunger is far beyond wanting something roasted in delectable marinade.

Half the world is hungry. More than half. The wealthiest measure comfort by knowing they will never want, never need. Insanity rests here.

COVID-19 enters the melee. Pandemic parts swiftly, escalating despair, lack of staples, safety. Two months into lockdown, with a deranged billionaire megalomaniac at the helm, cities reboot in politically separate worlds. Willing to sacrifice "human capital stock" to the virus, for capital. Within days, in a pandemic, innocent black people are quickly murdered by police. In their beds, in their sleep, and walking down the street, until everyone has suffered seeing enough, until it all burns. Until, masked and gathered, the citizens speak. #BlackLivesMatter, they do.

Half the world is hungry. More. All the money in the world, and still, parting halves.

James Fowler

James Fowler is the author of *The Pain Trader* (Golden Antelope Press, 2020). A professor of English at the University of Central Arkansas, his teaching interests include Victorian literature, modern poetry, and science-based drama. In addition to scholarly articles, he writes short stories and personal essays. His thinking on economics has been influenced by Ruskin, Thoreau, Michael Moore, and the business section of the newspaper.

∿ *The School for Lucre*

Its endowment dazzles. Such big patrons.
Thanks to pharmaceuticals. Thanks to petrochemicals.
Thanks to hamburgers.

$$\$$$

In stock lab the students test rumors,
learn how to stampede nervous traders.

$$\$$$

The fiscal glee club practices scales:
dol-lar-di-nar-kro-na-eu-ro,
li-ra-ru-pee-ru-ble-pe-so.

$$\$$$

This year's Malthus Prize goes to Brian L.
for his paper, "Privatizing the Four Elements."

$$\$$$

The royal we is now the corporate we,
as in, "We are not amused
by your antitrust suit."

$$\$$$

In the realm of metafinance
imaginary resources fill inconceivable needs.

$$\$$$

The faculty has pegged the value of
human life, adjusted for inflation.

$$\$$$

To make a killing on cattle futures
one must know something the cattle don't.

$$\$$$

As field project, the hostile takeover:
Brad acquires a Quaker village;
Tiffany bags an eye bank.

$

A cornered market is a happy market.

$

As usual, the media gets it backward.
Professor P. proposed raising livestock
on processed human waste.

$

The campus Lothario woos unsuspecting
pension funds.

$

Vivid acting carries the spring melodrama.
The cruel EPA inspector is wickedly stringent.

$

According to dream theory, a sobbing man
in a suit represents poor investment.

$

The Efficiency Institute toys with a model
for sacking the entire workforce.

$

For amusement students play treacherous
zero-sum games.

$

Financial engineers proudly unveil the nillo,
a trading issue seven times removed
from any actual commodity.

$

Moola, the school's prestigious journal,
returns an article on the Federal Reserve's
subjection to the evil god Loki through
a wooden Indian in Glens Falls.
Basically, the research needs updating.

$

School officials commission a mural:
The Triumph of Business over Anti-Business.

$

Conferred with degrees of respectability,
ambitious graduates commence to lower
the bottom line.

From the Poet

I wrote "The School for Lucre" as a satire on business schools, which are a central fixture of the modern corporate university. Professional programs have featured prominently at the graduate level for well over a century, but they have now swamped the undergraduate curriculum too, some of their courses numbering even among general-education options. Higher ed these days seems less a matter of advanced intellectual pursuit than pricy vo-tech instruction. This is a common lament from the cornered liberal-arts sector, which must make a hard sell of its offerings to those students who view humane learning as a luxury at best.

What business majors with sugarplum visions of entrepreneurial success may fail to realize is how difficult it is to get a new venture off the ground. Rather than helming their own innovative start-up, they could well find themselves heavily indebted serfs in corporate America, struggling to keep their purchase on middle-class standing. Not having acquired the freethinking skills that could enable them to stand back and critique the economic system they were fed wholesale in school, they might see no recourse but to slog on in bitter pragmatism.

The poem itself, though, imagines the most crass and predatory of capitalist training camps. Its excesses may be fanciful—hence fun to write and read about—but periodic outrages on the business front should leave the public wondering just where rogue bankers, traders, and executives pick up their values and tricks. Could it be that schooling focused on money-making is a key link in a chain that leads to an insular, profit-bound corporate culture?

In case you're thinking, "Yeah, just another academic socialist spouting off from the comfort of tenured security," I'll say here that I'm not a fan of party-run communism, whose habitual sin has been to oppress people in the name of the people. Rather, I favor strictly regulated capitalism, with a healthy helping of social-welfare programs. Especially where big money is involved, I believe that a free market is sooner or later a corrupt market. Capitalism, like fire, has many uses when kept in check; unrestrained, it consumes rapaciously everything in its path until it burns itself out.

I subscribe to the common wisdom that it's good to have just enough money so that you don't have to think much about it. Too little, and you're constantly harassed by its shortage; too much, and you're probably scheming to get more, persuaded that there's no better means to keep score in life. Of course, capital does magnify influence and afford access to power in a way that labor can only seek to rival through collective action. But what happens to the individual will inflated by money, measuring its interests in the most material, increasingly aggressive ways, is not usually pretty.

Martín Espada

Martín Espada's latest collection of poems is *Floaters*
(W. W. Norton, 2021). Among his other books are *Vivas to Those
Who Have Failed* (W. W. Norton, 2016), *The Trouble Ball* (W. W. Norton,
2011), and *The Republic of Poetry* (W. W. Norton, 2006), which was a finalist
for the Pulitzer Prize. He has received the Ruth Lilly Poetry Prize, the
Shelley Memorial Award, the Robert Creeley Award, the National Hispanic
Cultural Center Literary Award, the PEN/Revson Fellowship, and a
Guggenheim Fellowship. A former tenant lawyer, Espada is a professor
of English at the University of Massachusetts Amherst.

∽ Who Burns for the Perfection of Paper

At sixteen, I worked after high school hours
at a printing plant
that manufactured legal pads:
yellow paper stacked seven feet high
and leaning
as I slipped cardboard
between the pages,
then brushed red glue
up and down the stack.
No gloves: fingertips required
for the perfection of paper,
smoothing the exact rectangle.
Sluggish by 9 PM, the hands
would slide along suddenly sharp paper,
and gather slits thinner than the crevices
of the skin, hidden.
Then the glue would sting,
hands oozing
till both palms burned
at the punch clock.

Ten years later, in law school,
I knew that every legal pad
was glued with the sting of hidden cuts,
that every open lawbook
was a pair of hands
upturned and burning.

∽ The Saint Vincent de Paul Food Pantry Stomp
Madison, Wisconsin, 1980

Waiting for the carton of food
given with Christian suspicion
even to agency-certified charity cases
like me,
thin and brittle

as uncooked linguini,
anticipating the factory-damaged cans
of tomato soup, beets, three-bean salad
in a welfare cornucopia,
I spotted a squashed dollar bill
on the floor, and with
a Saint Vincent de Paul food pantry stomp
pinned it under my sneaker,
tied my laces meticulously,
and stuffed the bill in my sock
like a smuggler of diamonds,
all beneath the plaster statue wingspan
of Saint Vinnie,
who was unaware
of the dance
named in his honor
by a maraca player
in the salsa band
of the unemployed.

ꙅ Offerings to an Ulcerated God
Chelsea, Massachusetts

Mrs. López refuses to pay rent,
and we want her out,
the landlord's lawyer said,
tugging at his law school ring.
The judge called for an interpreter,
but all the interpreters were gone,
trafficking in Spanish
at the criminal session
on the second floor.

A volunteer stood up in the gallery.
Mrs. López showed the interpreter
a poker hand of snapshots,
the rat curled in a glue trap
next to the refrigerator,

the water frozen in the toilet,
a door without a doorknob
(No rent for this. I know the law
and I want to speak,
she whispered to the interpreter).

Tell her she has to pay
and she has ten days to get out,
the judge commanded, rose
so the rest of the courtroom rose,
and left the bench. Suddenly
the courtroom clattered
with the end of business:
the clerk of the court
gathered her files
and the bailiff went to lunch.
Mrs. López stood before the bench,
still holding up her fan of snapshots
like an offering this ulcerated god
refused to taste,
while the interpreter
felt the burning
bubble in his throat
as he slowly turned to face her.

From the Poet

I wrote "Who Burns for the Perfection of Paper" based on my experience working at a printing plant in high school, where I made legal pads by hand. Ten years later, I ended up at Northeastern University Law School in Boston, surrounded by a sea of legal pads—and people who had no idea how legal pads were made. We take the labor of others for granted, the suffering that goes into the creation of everyday objects for our use. Neruda, in his "Ode to Salt," not only praised the salt but the labor that went into the salt, the suffering behind the salt. Here, there is literally blood in the glue—and a leap from the legal pads to the law books. The legal system, represented by the law books, is on fire. The hands "upturned and burning" speak to the suffering inherent in the law, which defends the owners of factories. The poem draws a line between invisible economic exploitation and the legal structure that supports and validates this system of exploitation.

And where better to learn about the emphasis on property over people than in court, with landlord-tenant cases? "Offerings to an Ulcerated God" came from my experience as an attorney and supervisor of Su Clínica Legal, a legal services program for low-income, Spanish-speaking people in Chelsea, Massachusetts. I witnessed in court the machinery of the law protecting property and the owners of property. To that end, legal language works to obscure, rather than clarify; to control, rather than communicate. As such, the language of the law has great power to disorient its victims. That disorientation becomes dizziness for those victims of the court system twice removed from legal language because of the inability to speak English. I found myself serving not only as attorney but translator. Once, I volunteered in court to interpret for a woman who was not my client; that became the genesis of the poem.

My professor and mentor at the University of Wisconsin, Herbert Hill, would make a distinction between "clients" and "constituents." I have been both a client and a constituent. "The Saint Vincent de Paul Food Pantry Stomp" documents a moment in my life when I had dropped out of school, ended up unemployed, and was certified indigent by a social service organization in Madison. That organization referred me to Saint Vinnie's, where, for whatever reason, they doubted my veracity. While they mulled over my fate, I saw a stray dollar bill on the floor, stamped it with my foot, and stuffed it in my sock. I needed the dollar, but I also needed the gesture of defiance. Years later, I wrote the poem; one of the great benefits of being a poet is the opportunity for revenge.

Jo Pitkin

Jo Pitkin is the author of three volumes of poetry: *Rendering* (Salmon Poetry, 2017), *Commonplace Invasions* (Salmon Poetry, 2014), and *Cradle of the American Circus: Poems from Somers, New York* (The History Press, 2012). In 2017, Pitkin received a grant from the Barbara Deming Memorial Fund to work on her current project, *Village: Recession* (Salmon Poetry, 2020). Pitkin lives in New York's Hudson Valley, where she works as a freelance educational writer.

ᔆ Village: Closure

Even the divine feels the pinch.

In this week's local paper,
the treasurer announced the closing
of the white clapboard church on the hill
after 177 years of weekly worship.

No one mows the spires of grass.

Inside, collection plates gleam
like a row of full moons
on a winter night.

ᔆ Village: Food Chain

> Oh yes, you see the mice set up the whole Earth business, as an epic
> experiment in behavioural psychology.
> —DOUGLAS ADAMS, *The Hitchhiker's Guide to the Galaxy*

Field mice swarm for crumbs & scraps.

Three black rat snakes seek their succulence.

A pair of hawks swoops down for snake supper.

Once they fly off, the plumber, carpenter, electrician,

exterminator, the butcher, the baker, & candlestick maker

bolt, nail, caulk my home with pointed tools. Here, at the top,

I worry. How to pay for all this water, this shelter, this heat, this light.

ᔆ Village: Can Collector

Nina rummages rows of clattery bins,
tosses nickel deposit bottles & cans
into her dented green minivan.

Each week she takes home sixty dollars,
one hundred when during summers
the village parched drink more.

Her cramped concrete porch muddles
clothes, books, toys, dishes, tables,
a 24-hour yard sale spring to fall.

She won't fret the current recession.
Foraging discards is her obsession.
The cans?—they'll pay for gas

around Arizona where she winters
and reads Ishiguro & Michener
in an adobe she built herself

on her own five acres.

～ Village: White Money

Every Wednesday this winter
snowstorms piled more snow
on chalky, constricted streets.
Our part-time snowplow driver
doesn't complain. He just pushes
and pushes dirty banks higher
under starlight and moonlight,
spreads sand and salt like icing
on an asphalt cake, patrols roads
alone in a cramped mile-high cab
with two headlamps and steel.
He works when we are asleep.
He eats farm breakfasts—grits,
eggs, ham, sausage—at midnight,
closes his eyes for a bit at noon.
I don't mind, George declares
behind the wheel of his tall blue
truck with a banged-up scraper.
It's all good. It's white money.

From the Poet

The four poems in *The Poetry of Capital* are part of *Village: Recession*. My project came about in response to the financial crisis that began in 2007. As a self-employed, single woman in the book publishing industry, I felt the economic downturn keenly. For decades, I had supported myself as a freelance educational writer creating student books, teacher's guides, and ancillaries for kindergarten through twelfth-grade students. But beginning in 2008, I found myself struggling to earn a living. The career I had worked so hard to build seemed to be vanishing. Rates dropped. Work dried up. Companies folded. And I had no fallback plan.

As the recession deepened, I eventually turned to a new project as a way to deal with my feelings of anxiety, frustration, and disappointment. With paying work scarce, I reveled in a rare block of unscheduled time. What better way to combat the recession than by writing my way through it—and *about* it? I decided to explore the effects of the Great Recession through the focused lens of the tiny village where I live. This setting afforded me an intimate vantage point from which to document personal experiences as well as those of friends and neighbors like Nina, the redeemable bottle and can collector, and George, the snow plower.

While the poems in *Village: Recession* focus on the difficulties of the Great Recession, I also derived inspiration from the chronicles of members of my own family—whether they had faced the hardships of immigration in the 1650s or the catastrophic Great Depression of the 1930s. The poems also touch on the different ways in which we are sustained during a rough patch. Throughout the economic crisis of the late 2000s—and again during the global coronavirus pandemic in 2020—I found solace in small acts of kindness and momentary relief from isolation and uncertainty in everyday encounters with villagers and the natural world.

Kimiko Hahn

Kimiko Hahn's most recent book, *Foreign Bodies* (W. W. Norton, 2020), was prompted by hoarding and consumption, and the way objects can possess us. The collection's three long poems are based on outside source material in much the same way that the poet's previous work was triggered by Asian American identity, women's issues, entomology, and black lung disease. She is a distinguished professor in the MFA Program in Creative Writing and Literary Translation at Queens College, CUNY.

∼ Things That Remind Me of Squalor
after Sei Shonagon

The jacket of a chain-smoker. 14th St. subway station. H said, Stephen
Crane's "Maggie: A Girl of the Streets." People who tie dogs up outdoors,
in any season.

For Esmé—With Love and Squalor

Sei Shonagon

termites

Ed Gein's kitchen (Hoarder that he was. And a necrophile.) (But why that
coffee can of chewed-up gum?)

termite eggs

skin-heads

(But is Hank the 3rd a skin-head—or just his guitarist who kept hitting
his head with the mic until a gash gushed up blood?)

eBay: *Occupied Japan Doll "little black boy holding watermelon and sitting
on potty."* This is the worst I've seen. The "Oriental" ones are either sweet
or creepy (and sweet) and, oddly, rarely dressed in kimono. The "Eskimo"
or "Indian" salt-n-pepper shakers are cute, too. I bought two "black
babies" in cloth diapers which I find charming—but H said *please keep
that in your study and don't show them to anyone.* I don't know. All possess a
racist aspect, but does that make me a racist? I don't know.

The Savage Nation

Flint tap water

A stone disturbed, ants scurry around to carry off their eggs.

∼ Constant Objection

More often than not, a house fills up
with only stifled objections
to a dozen glue-guns, a case of Brillo pads,

jars of preserves. But—coffee cans
of chewed up chewing gum?

*

Notice that the simplest often yields the most:
object: body, stuff, organism, meaning, purpose,
idea, hope, butt, doodad, . . . mind and *resist.*
A theory as well: Pinky-Bear,
Blankie, Sock-Puppet, Nightmare.

*

Objection? Outside a neighboring clinic
three fundamentalists wait
to shoot the doctor at point-blank range.
Meantime, Father saw Medusa
on the clothesline, under the sink,
in a tureen of string beans.

*

He drew the ball of curly alive hair
that no one can stand or he'll turn to stone.
Then there's cherry-red on her toes.
Then there's his own weekend Father
taking him to "Boxing Kangaroos"
who turned out to be yawning strippers.

*

Objectification! Marx wrote:
As values, all commodities are only
definite masses of congealed labour time.
Yes, Hamburger-Helper, trombone, robot vacuum!

Yes, covert kiwi or flagrant heroin!
(Coffee can of chewed-up chewing gum—
was just a murderer's odd penchant.)

*

Before tossing her clothes and cosmetics
I crisscrossed the city on a bus:

peering out at the concrete,
cherry blossoms fell in my hair
from no open window. They piped up,
How much more can a daughter object?

From the Poet

Japanese poetics have imbued my poetry at least from my undergraduate days, when I was studying Japanese literature with great passion. One characteristic is the use of words with multiple meanings. So, for me, "object" became a portal into inner and outer spaces. I love to see where I am led as I play with, say, the noun and verb, or knowledge, intimate and public.

Another attraction to Japanese poetics is form. For "Things That . . .," the form is the zuihitsu. (The best examples can be found in *The Pillow Book of Sei Shonagon*.) My own appear as a catalog of what comes to mind when I hear the word "squalor." For "Constant Objection," I explore the kind of juxtaposing that I experience reading tanka.

While studying Japanese literature in graduate school, I was also leafleting outside factory gates. I think the issue was the Taft-Hartley Act. And I was the tenant organizer for our funky building. (Years later, the professional organizer who guided me through court legalities was murdered by a gang.) And I met my future husband at meetings and performances for Artists Call Against U.S. Intervention in Central America.

What a time to cut one's political teeth. What a time to be *lyrical*. This is where dialectics has taken me.

David Baker

David Baker is the author of twelve books of poetry, including
Swift: New and Selected Poems (W. W. Norton, 2019) and *Never-Ending
Birds* (W. W. Norton, 2009), which was awarded the Theodore Roethke
Memorial Poetry Prize. His six books of prose include *Seek After:
Essays on Seven Modern Lyric Poets* (Steve F. Austen, 2018). He holds
the Thomas B. Fordham Chair at Denison University and is the
poetry editor of *The Kenyon Review*.

∿ Midwest: Ode

You could believe a life so plain it means
calmness in the lives of others, who come
to see it, hold it, buy it piece by piece,
as these good people easing from their van
onto the curb where the big-shoed children
of Charm, Ohio, have lined their baskets
of sweet corn, peaches, and green beans.
Each Saturday morning the meeting point
of many worlds is a market in Charm.

You could believe a name so innocent
it is accurate and without one blade
of irony, and green grass everywhere.
Yet, how human a pleasure the silk hairs
when the corn is peeled back, and the moist worm
curls on the point of an ear like a tongue—
how charged the desire of the children who
want to touch it, taste it, turn it over,
until it has twirled away in the dust.

There are black buggies piled high with fruit pies.
There are field things hand-wrought of applewood
and oak, and oiled at the palm of one man.
There are piecework quilts black-striped and maroon
and mute as dusk, and tatting, and snow shawls,
and cozies the colors of prize chickens—
though the corporate farm five miles away
has made its means of poultry production
faster, makes fatter hens, who need to sleep,

so machinery rumbles the nights through.
Still, it is hard to tell who lives with
more placid curiosity than these,
not only the bearded men in mud boots
and city kids tugging on a goat rope,
but really the whole strange market of Charm,
Ohio, where weekly we come, who stare
and smile at each other, to weigh the short
business end of a dollar in our hands.

∿ Postmodernism

The scene you loathe, the sheer fervor, the speed
   of the dangerous cabs—the city street
in oil, in spray when they pass, and the white
   exhaustion of the passersby like clouds.

You've been fired or you're on your way to work.
   If you're reading this it doesn't matter.
What matters is you're wet, and hurrying
   or hungry, or not, or in no hurry

whatsoever. It's almost this easy.
   When you duck inside the café doorway,
the body smell of the animal stone,
   to find a little shelter, there's your face

like a face in the plate-glass sheet and door.
   There's the wealthy hungry seated inside.
On the other side, past the entrance, the rained-
   out passageway of air and stone, bombed-out

crapped-out building in a husk of smoke, there's
   the junkie, coughing on her cardboard flat.
You see because you see the reflection
   in the big glass, your face like an etching

between them, a breath, or a sudden change
   of venue. It's too convenient even
for art or argument—are you hungry?
   is she a junkie?—all of you framed for

an instant like a political ad.
   No one is looking at anyone else.
The street surges, it chokes, but you're caught there.
   And now even your pity is worthless.

From the Poet

"Postmodernism" and "Midwest: Ode": do these poems depict two separate scenes? Or perhaps they are essentially the same scene in two different settings.

"Postmodernism" takes place in an urban location—a glassy, fancy restaurant along a familiar contemporary block. That is, there's a chic café right next door to a "bombed-out crapped-out" remnant of a building, a ruin. Proximity is the central circumstance here. I find irony—what Harold Bloom defines as "the clash of incommensurate forces"—in the edge-effect of things, where one community, one circumstance, butts up directly against a radically different community or circumstance. That's where the heat is and, for me, the productive dramatic tension. It's where you find all the friction, the energy, and the trouble.

Here, the wealthy patrons are in immediate proximity to the destitute woman. Only the sheet of glass separates them, like a television screen or the wall of a fish tank. And reflected on that screen, on either side, is the "you" of the poem, the reader, perhaps the poet. I hope, looking each way, all ways, that there's horror in a scene of such easy luxury and such heart-breaking pain. It's a scene I find in big cities, always—such radical and proximate inequity. Power and money rubbing shoulders with sacrifice, pain, and sorrow. A relative few possess unspeakable wealth and privilege, and so many have nothing. In fact, those few have built their wealth directly on top of the many.

The figure of "you" appears in "Midwest: Ode," too. At first, I think, this poem seems to present a very different scene from "Postmodernism." It's clearly more pastoral, or at least more rural, compared to the smoldering urbanness of the other. But the edge-effect is identical. It's "the meeting point of many worlds." The city people have come to the charming village to buy the wares of the country people with their big shoes and plain ways. All sides ogle each other, even as the "you" becomes the "we."

The largest population of Amish people in the world is located in central Ohio, mostly in Holmes County, one county away from mine. The farms are gorgeous and expansive, worked by tractors and animal-teams alike; the houses are spic-and-span, generally unencumbered by power lines and phone poles. Buggies alongside pickups alongside SUVs. The villages tend to be just as practical and "plain" as the farms. But the village of Charm, Ohio, and one or two more, serve the Amish by catering to outsiders, to the

"English." These places are overtly touristy with their knickknacks and kitsch, their bountiful bakeries and field stands, woolen mills, "authentic" clothing shops, and such.

Wordsworth knew the sorrow of "getting and spending." That sorrow happens—big city, little village—when our only real point of contact is the passing back and forth of money.

Joseph Gastiger

Joseph Gastiger taught for many years at Northern Illinois
University before attending Chicago Theological Seminary and then
becoming a pastor in DeKalb at First Congregational UCC in 2001.
He has published two collections of prose poems, *Loose Talk* (2012)
and *If You So Desire* (2014), both with Lost Horse Press.

∿ The Industrial Age

Before all the plants died, my father worked for Hoffman Beverage, went
out on road calls to Pelham to crawl under broken-down vans. Maybe a
ball joint had busted, maybe a clutch gave out. He'd set up flares and crawl
under the cab—getting it wrong half of the time, swearing at bolts,
stubbing out Camels, scared he'd be fired. We didn't know. Not until,
finally, Hoffman went broke—went off the highway, right through a
guardrail, in his new car. I remember the soda pop tower just off the
Garden State around Newark, there at the bottling plant where he took
me once when he was happy, no idea why—maybe I asked. Thousands of
bottles rattling along on conveyer belts, pulleys and chains—filling with
cherry and cola, sarsaparilla and ginger—swiveling past, caps getting
stamped on with a pneumatic hiss. One by one, they got sorted into
crates, workers stacking the pallets a forklift would carry out to the docks.
That's how I figured the world got made—hand grenades, cigarettes,
bazookas, toys, jars of Noxzema for my older sister, canned lima beans.
All rolling past, empty containers filling with everything there ever was,
sealed with a hiss, carted to neighborhood groceries that haven't existed
for years, almost as lost as Crusader Rabbit and poor Tinker Tom. Part of
me, still, wanted to drop out of school, to live and die wearing coveralls—
smelling the salt marsh, sulfur, syrup, and grease. Part of me grieved it
was already gone.

∿ Parable of Untraceable Power
for the Koch Brothers

From cell towers in Curaçao, laptops in Lebanon, smartphones in
Singapore and Macau, wavelets of dark money crisscross the Gulf
Stream, Indian Ocean, South China Sea. Some of it flows through your
muscle and bone—micro-bursts of profit and loss from the traffic in
ivory, blood diamonds, young girls, rhinoceros horn. Dark money
deepens the flavor of wine; betrays one general, embraces another;
infiltrates tax codes and textbooks as it circulates through the xylem and
phloem of clouds. Traveling at speeds you can't even imagine, dark money
pulses from Riyadh to Houston, Zurich to Tokyo, your bank to mine,
encrypting/decrypting whose city will burn, whose child go hungry, for
how long, and why.

∽ Hamelin

Rats tumbling from drainpipes and nesting wherever they couldn't be found. Masses were said, beggars were flogged, to no avail. Half the hotels shut down. Breweries closed. That's when the piper came, wearing a tattered rainbow, too good to be true. Pay him a thousand florins, he said, and he'd kill all the rats before the market stalls opened at dawn. And once they shouted yes, then he began to play a tune they thought they knew, but weren't sure. Rats ran from sacks of grain, out of the choir lofts, out of the monks' cells and latrines. And the piper played on, skirling until the last of them hurtled headlong into the greasy river and drowned. That's when the shopkeepers, setting out turnips, hats, and hams, made up their minds fifty florins should be enough. Which the piper wouldn't take. Too bad for you, he didn't quite say, with true reluctance and regret. Many who just a few hours before would've paraded him all over town grumbled, he must be an Indian sorcerer. He fled. But that same night, while each one slept, the piper filled the square with a more wonderful, more potent song. A song which no mother could hear, but which woke every child, prickled the air with a longing to be gone. So they crept out of bed, pattered in silence, one by one, called by the piper down the Street of No Drums. And he led them away, all but the blind girl and the crippled boy who lagged behind. You can believe, as others do, a mountainside parted somehow—wavered like water and, after they'd sleepwalked in, closed up again. You can believe they marched off on a children's crusade and were lost. But that doesn't explain why they'd keep reappearing—behind a loom, maybe, in Bridgeport or slapping mud into bricks in the heat outside Lahore. It doesn't explain why one washes ashore while another does flips for coins. Why another turns up in a ditch along the Jersey Turnpike, a duffel bag in the snow. For a thousand florins—the price of an oil well, a casino, or a cloud—one might ransom all the children of Hamelin. Yet no one will pay.

From the Poet

I grew up with my parents and sisters and crazy grandmother in a cramped house in a working-class Long Island neighborhood. I was always made aware, not consciously but through looks and sighs, that money was tight.

Any big, unplanned expense—fixing the furnace, for instance—could make my mother cry.

My father was a mechanic who, as he got older, worried a lot about losing his job, and sometimes did. My mother worked, as well—in lunchrooms and movie theatres and, later on, in steel and glass banks. People in my part of town didn't count on going to college.

All of this shaped my sense of what money is, where it comes from, how people earn it, and what it can do. These prose poems evoke three phases of my understanding.

"The Industrial Age" speaks of a time when I assumed going to work meant punching in at some plant where people ran huge machines producing consumer goods. And, as these goods were shipped, bought, and consumed, a tiny slice of what they sold for became the workers' pay. I didn't think about labor and management, or venture capital—not as a scruffy kid walking to school. I didn't really consider corporate power and its effect on the world until I started going to Vietnam War protests in seventh grade.

Today, money's no longer tethered to commodities or to things we can see or touch. Capital has become an almost ghostly shape-changing force, able to topple regimes, create dynasties, or leave millions hungry. It flits through cyberspace, decreeing from day to day not just how much or little we know but what *can* become known. That is the terror and wonder behind my second prose poem, "Parable."

Finally, in "Hamelin," I revisit the tale of the pied piper, a story that's haunted me much of my life. It's a warning about what is likely to go wrong when holding on to wealth becomes our highest concern. A society intoxicated by greed is likely to enslave the children of strangers. Sooner or later, it may devour its own children, too.

Tony Hoagland

Tony Hoagland was the author of eight poetry collections,
including *Priest Turned Therapist Treats Fear of God* (Graywolf, 2018)
and *What Narcissism Means to Me* (Graywolf, 2003), a finalist for the
National Book Critics Circle Award. He also published two collections
of essays, including *Twenty Poems That Could Save America and Other
Essays* (Graywolf, 2014). He received the O. B. Hardison Prize for
Poetry and Teaching from the Folger Shakespeare Library, the Poetry
Foundation's Mark Twain Award, and the Jackson Poetry Prize.
Hoagland died in October 2018.

∽ America

Then one of the students with blue hair and a tongue stud
Says America is for him a maximum-security prison whose walls

Are made of Radio Shacks and Burger Kings, and MTV episodes
Where you can't tell the show from the commercials;

And as I contemplate how full of shit I think he is,
He says that even when he's driving to the mall in his Isuzu

Trooper with a gang of his friends, letting rap music pour over them
Like a boiling Jacuzzi full of ball peen hammers, even then he feels

Buried alive, captured and suffocated in the folds
Of the thick satin quilt of America.

And I wonder if this is a legitimate category of pain,
Or whether he is just spin-doctoring a better grade,

And then I remember that when I stabbed my father in the dream last
    night,
It was not blood but money

That gushed out of him, bright green hundred-dollar bills
Spilling from his wounds, and—this is the funny part—

He gasped, "Thank God—those Ben Franklins were
Clogging up my heart—

And so I perish happily,
Freed from that which kept me from my liberty"—

Which is when I knew it was a dream, since my dad
Would never speak in rhymed couplets.

And I look at the student with his acne and cell phone and phony ghetto
    clothes
And I think, "I am asleep in America too,

And I don't know how to wake myself either."
And I remember what Marx said near the end of his life:

"I was listening to the cries of the past,
When I should have been listening to the cries of the future."

But how could he have imagined 100 channels of 24-hour cable
Or what kind of nightmare it might be

When each day you watch rivers of bright merchandise run past you
And you are floating in your pleasure boat upon this river

Even while others are drowning underneath you
And you see their faces twisting in the surface of the waters

And yet it seems to be your own hand
Which turns the volume higher?

∿ Big Grab

The corn chip engineer gets a bright idea,
and talks to the corn chip executive
and six months later at the factory they begin subtracting
a few chips from every bag,

but they still call it on the outside wrapper,
The Big Grab,
so the concept of Big is quietly modified
to mean *More or Less Large, or Only Slightly Less Big than Before.*

Confucius said this would happen:
that language would be hijacked and twisted
by a couple of tricksters from the Business Department

and from then on words would get crookeder and crookeder
until no one would know how to build a staircase,
or to look at the teeth of a horse,
or when it is best to shut up.

We live in that time that he predicted.
Nothing means what it says,
and it says it all the time.
Out on route 28, the lights blaze all night
on a billboard of a beautiful girl
covered with melted cheese—

See how she beckons to the river of late-night cars;
See how the tipsy drivers swerve, under the breathalyzer moon!

We're in the wilderness now,
confused by the signs,
with a shortness of breath,
and that postmodern feeling of falling behind.

In a story whose beginning I must have missed,
without a name for the thing
                    I can barely comprehend I desire,
I speak these words that do not know
where they're going.

No wonder I want something more-or-less large,
and salty for lunch.
No wonder I stare into space while eating it.

From the Poet

Isn't it strange that we human beings have dreams of *money*, in the same
way that we have dreams about food and sex? It shows how much of our
animal nature has been replaced, or displaced, by alien imaginaries, until
we think and breathe in what amounts to a different language. Think of the
TV show, or movie, in which some stockbroker, banker, or bank robber says
theatrically that the footlocker full of hundred-dollar bills "is making me
hard," or, "All those zeros are making me wet." I wonder, does that really
happen? And I bet that it does.

The problems with capital and its giant mommy, Capitalism, aren't
inherent. Where things go wrong is when one system of value pushes all
the other systems out of existence. So the value of money can displace the
values of love, family, nature, the pleasure of drinking wine in the back
yard. Or at least, it can push those values out of our heads and, therefore,
out of our lives. Then these other reasons for living—charity, courage,
mercy, storytelling, service, brotherhood—lose their primacy in competi-
tion with the triumphant invasive system.

Of course, I'm not an economist but a citizen writer. Yet I believe a few
things. Poetry has a place in the culture of our time because it reminds us
of the other things we live for: the deep roots of our consciousness and

creatureliness. A poem rehydrates the imagination and the emotions of the person who reads or hears it. In this magical way, it can restore the order of our reasons for living.

Secondly—and perhaps this is a matter of personal inclination—I feel that poetry mustn't ignore the glittering, violent, denatured, insulting actualities of the modern world. Poetry can and should incorporate hedge fund managers, Viagra factories, climate change, high heels, the lies told by politicians, Somali immigrants in inner tubes on the Red Sea, and yoga teachers eating Fig Newtons at midnight. A poem can gather the world into its frame, illuminate its glorious beautiful catastrophes, and do the work of meaning-making with those materials. Poetry must not become cloistered, overly esoteric, and precious. Poetry is tough, it can get angry, and it can take on what needs taking on, including the many-headed Hydras of history and capitalism.

David Wojahn

David Wojahn's nine collections of poetry include *For the Scribe*
(University of Pittsburgh Press, 2017) and *Interrogation Palace:*
New and Selected Poems 1982–2004 (University of Pittsburgh Press,
2006), a named finalist for the Pulitzer Prize and winner of the
O. B. Hardison Award. Wojahn is also the author of two collections of
essays. He is a professor of English at Virginia Commonwealth
University and on the faculty of the MFA program of
Vermont College of the Fine Arts.

∾ Ghost Mall: Richmond, Virginia

That the JCPenney is now a house of prayer: pad-locked accordion gate,
    metal chairs in rows surrounding
service desks, cash registers unbolted & gone. That a wooden riser makes
    a kind of altar, its cross of unlit neon,
amps & keyboard, a podium pulpit. That Luke is in a mood, his freshly
    purchased Nikes notwithstanding,

trying to pick the padlock with a paper clip before I yank him
    past the patron-less Hallmark shop,
soft pretzel stand with its kid in headphones, dozing behind the counter.
    That from 7 screens
inside the Chik-fil-a, the President gloats & lies. Our mission:
    bags for the Hoover from the former

Sharper Image, now a purveyor of used vacuums (*cash only no card or check*).
    Storefront after storefront shuttered.
That the closed HQ of the Libertarians sports a pile of unused lawn signs.
    That one could procure
tattoos, crystal meth & pedicures. That Luke could have picked the lock
    in seconds. That de Tocqueville,

in 1826, identified America's two sole passions: the need to be free
    & the need to be led.
3 levels of escalators, most broken down. Outside, the light is blinding
    & we've gone to the wrong side
of the parking lot, the empty cordoned-off expanse, where the re-enactors
    swelter in their butternut,

uniforms sewn in sweat shops in Macao or Bangladesh.
    The Lost Cause-ers
pacing or sprawling in lounge chairs, muskets propped beside them.
    That Luke wants some video,
though I warn him to keep his cell in his pocket. A pickup flares
    the Stars & Bars. The bumper stickers

hiss like Miltonic snakes. They are here to rehearse next week's
    performance of Pickett's Charge.
A few dozen chiropractors, CPAs & car dealers—standing in for 11,000
    bayonet-flashing troops.

They slink across the asphalt in formation, muskets pointed outward
    toward a pair of food trucks

representing Little Round Top & its Yankee cannons. Closer, closer,
    drumbeat, another 50 yards
& for an instant they are charging—then falling primly to their knees.
    Shouts from the little crowd
& it all begins anew. That de Tocqueville belittled patriotism: "never more
    than an extension of individual egotism."

Next week, says the woman in her lounge chair, petting the barking
    Yorkie on her lap,
they will all die again at the real Gettysburg, real cannon, the killing field
    confounded with smoke.
Luke snaps photos of Generals Longstreet & Pettigrew, who seem
    to be comparing battle sabers.

That in the Oval Office, another "executive order" is signed.
    That Little Round Top
reverts to its taco-truck avatar, a pair of kegs to be untapped.
    Thy vanity, thy vanity, how shall
we pull it down? That the soldiery has risen from the asphalt & its white
    diagonal parking grids.

That they dust off their gray woolen knees, muskets shouldered as they
    yammer at their cells. For the cause
of mammon, for the cause of human chattel, for the cause of
    remembrance,
    of bitter benighted history
which *must live with what was here.* That they rise again. They rise.
    Always the bastards rise again.

⌒ *Piñata*

This was a holiday party, after all, everyone a little buzzed,
the department office desks & computer screens bedecked
with Santas, oversize cardboard candy canes, a plastic

scrawny pine adorning the reception area desk
with its neatly stacked *Chronicles of Higher Ed*,
pinned-up dust jackets of faculty books. Imagine it,

dear reader. The eggnog had been replaced by harder
& more palatable fare. Ties loosened, heels removed
& stowed beneath the workstations. It was Culture Studies

Eddie who brought the President in,
assisted by Mona (long Eighteenth Century). Laughs
from everyone. Someone said he looked like Grendel

in an ill-fitting three-piece: his glower & the orange
confetti hair, seething like nature-show footage:
sea anemones, gyrating legs of upturned beetles.

They hung him by the neck, having strung
extension cords from the ceiling fluorescents.
The lottery to play the part of Lord High Executioner

(proceeds to the ACLU) had been won by Carol
the Medievalist, who'd taught here since the days
of Nixon and Kent State. She whispered some lines

from the Pardoner's Tale, as the Chair tied
her blindfold, admonishing her not to peek. Then
the Louisville Slugger—she smiled as we placed it in her hands.

We spun her & she took her reeling aim, grazing him
against the shoulder & he twisted & pendulum-ed,
careening against the copier. Always the age demands

an image, O reader, a grimace, a subterfuge,
a public lie. Another swipe or two & now the Xbox moment
when the kill is nigh, the shoulder gaping open,

temple parting to ooze a stream
of gold-foiled chocolate coins. A direct hit now
to the face: Tootsie Rolls, plastic whistles, shredded

newspaper, inching like larvae from where the nose
had been, the Cheeto-colored hair sailing down
in a feeble ticker tape parade. *You Go Girl*

squealed Loni the Dickinson scholar as Carol
tugged off the blindfold, landing one square in his crotch.
For the *coup de grâce*, Carol changed tactics, running the bat

through the center of his chest, like Plath impaling
her vampire Daddy. I am sorry, reader, that the YouTube
footage does not give this proper justice. Now he was shards

& wire & malted milk balls on linoleum, everyone circling
the scene, the Maenads of the College of Humanities & Science
awakened from their ecstasies to survey the flayed,

dismembered Pentheus. Plastic drink cups, mushrooms
stuffed with goat cheese & fennel. Soon it would be time
to pick up kids from soccer, to check on mothers

in Assisted Living. In a factory in Oaxaca, the workers
are assembling the President's successors. Tina & Alana,
13 & 11, have all day glued orange confetti to the paper skulls.

Marta with a fine horsehair brush over & over paints
the scowl & feral eyes & Manuel & Tomaz, since 5 this morning,
have stirred a cauldron of paper mache paste, careful to make

their molds exact. A warren of basement rooms, music from
a dozen radios, $2.50 a day. A buyer's being shown the wares,
the President's displayed in small, medium & *grande*.

& Manuel & Tomaz at the loading dock, stacking
200 *grandes* on an open pick-up bed, engine idling.
Now the journey north, with a burlap tarp tied snugly

to protect each sneering POTUS from the dust & sun.
The tarp: I had hoped to liken it to a burial shroud.
But that, dear reader, would be yet another lie.

From the Poet

I think of "Piñata" and "Ghost Mall: Richmond, Virginia" as something like
a diptych. The two poems derive from the experience of living through
what may be a pivotal time in our culture—the beginning of what could be
called the Era of Trump, an era that normalizes and endorses all manner of

injustice, misogyny, racism, and greed; an era which each day seems to bring a new bewilderment, be it the COVID-19 pandemic or the slaying of George Floyd. I want my poetry in general, and these two poems in particular, to raise a voice against this trend, yet do so in a way that avoids the sloganeering and agit-prop which too often characterizes "political poetry."

I tend to favor narrative in my poems, and both of the poems that appear here feature that. But I am always interested in what happens in a poem when two or more narrative motifs collide or conjoin. In the case of "Piñata," it's the story of an academic office party conflated with the lives of impoverished Mexican sweatshop workers; in the case of "Ghost Mall," it's an anecdote about my son and me visiting a dying shopping mall which gives way to an encounter with Civil War re-enactors. The times require a poetry of resistance. But that poetry can take many forms, addressing our national emergency in ways that can sometimes be direct and sometimes be slantwise: my two poems take the latter approach.

Mark Doty

Mark Doty's nine books of poems include *My Alexandria* (University
of Illinois, 1993), which won the National Book Critics Circle Award, and
Fire to Fire: New and Selected Poems (Harper Perennial, 2009), winner of
the National Book Award. His five volumes of nonfiction prose include
Dog Years (Harper Perennial, 2008), a *New York Times* bestseller.
He's taught at Columbia, NYU, Princeton, and Stanford. Currently
Distinguished Professor at Rutgers, he lives in New York City.

∾ *Air Rights*

The French Church—red brick,
    never much on looks, leaning
        in the direction of Romanesque—

settled into modest circumstances
    how many decades on W 16th?
        Nothing divine in the details,

veneer peeling from doors never
    meant for here, never open: no light,
        evenings, through colored glass,

though by day you could make out,
    twenty feet above the sidewalk,
        Christ stepping onto the waters

of Galilee, sea and savior oiled by exhaust,
    nearly indistinguishable. Weeknights
        lamps burned downstairs,

where a dozen groups renounced at length
    alcohol or crystal, skin or smoke,
        and what each circle resisted glowed

at the center of their ring of chairs,
    almost visible. There you could consecrate
        relinquishment, or find someone

already ruined to pursue whatever made you,
    for the night, unsinkable. The coins collected
        each time they passed the hat kept the church

afloat. Of the congregation, eight souls
    remained, Haitian evangelicals. Only once
        did I see someone mount the stairs

toward those slapdash doors
    —who could have missed her?
        Under a plane tree clearly considering

giving up all ambition, an idling Town Car's
    rear door opened, she stepped out,
        and I knew at once that if she'd ever

for a moment been thwarted, she simply
    summoned more of some alloy of metal and will
        she drew up from beneath the pavement,

maybe from Haiti itself, from generations
    that stood unbending in her, compromising
        with nothing. In her green hat,

in the forgiving archways of her green dress,
    her capacious purse, she conquered the stairs
        and raised her hand to open the door.

Just once. The meeting schedule disappeared
    from the basement entry's wire-gridded glass,
        the rooms stayed dark, addicts no longer

smoking and talking under the miserable tree.
    Twilights, before they were gone, I'd walk
        through a climate so thick I could almost

taste it, meet the gaze of men whose eyes locked
    into mine. Was this the night they knew
        was coming, the night they'd fall?

I recognized them, I wanted to put my hand
    into the wound at their sides,
        that we might be real to one another.

A barrier went up around the entry, papered
    with signs and permits, an "artist's rendering"
        descended out of the blue: fourteen stories

clad in bluestone, suspended above
    the freshened brick of the dwarfed church.
        A flyer in our vestibule said they'd sold

the space between their sanctuary
    and heaven for a cool eight million, and units
        in what would be the highest stepped-back

Nineveh tower on our block: raise the faithful high,
    plunge the neighbors into shadow.
        Lord thou preparest a banquet for me . . .

Workers boxed the plane tree's trunk
    in a cage of 2 × 4s, heavy equipment scooped
        a new foundation, hammered the pilings in.

How do they stand it, in Cairo or Rome,
    when any shaft in sand reaches down
        five thousand years? Bad enough in New York:

artifacts of quarantine and revolt,
    bullets that did or didn't strike the rioters,
        squatters or immigrants, Irish or black,

cemetery slabs etched with the hex of David's star,
    oyster middens, pipe-stems, earthenware
        stamped with eagles and shields.

And in the Historical Society, dug from a site
    like this one, the object I can't forget,
        plutonium half-life still ticking,

nightmare thing: brass shackles, finely made,
    locked into place by a brass bar,
        sized to fit the wrists of a child.

That sign the angel placed outside
    of Eden, forbidding re-entry?
        No arrow, but these joined zeroes

fetched up out of the mud,
    though their poison goes on
        seeping into the water table.

The backhoe clawed, rebar spiked
    its way up, and some days traffic stopped
        while the concrete mixer's big rotating drum

poured into place more of the substance
    of our block. The city stopped work more than once.
        I saw, where they'd poured the footing

a little short, workers float a three-inch layer
    along the foundation-top: sure to crack,
        perhaps one day to bring the whole thing down?

Though walking home, after hours, late winter,
    I found towering at the center of the night
        what seemed a vertical representation of heaven,

stacked episodes of the exaltations of light
    —a model of the spirit's progress,
        a pilgrim ladder, and where did it lead?

Unfinished, a swath of black netting
    veiling the lamps left burning within,
        that building would never be so beautiful again.

Up there, above the streets, might not desire
    be articulated, spoken till seen through?
        Now the Bradford pears open against

scaffolding crowning the new Barney's
    down the block, and black girders sketch out
        more floors above a French Church caged

in spars of steel, wave-walking Jesus shadowed
    by bristling supports above. Do the faithful
        look up toward a future in a world of light,

more square feet? More power to them
    if they do; who doesn't want a privacy to fill,
        or the luxury of amplitude, room for the self

to billow out in dreaming? The shadow
    pooling in my street's grown cooler,
        gained in depth. Sometimes I walk

a city block and notice that everyone's looking
    at a screen, or talking to someone who's somewhere else,
        so that *here* seems to thin out,

dispersed and characterless. I miss the addicts
    —you understand I've done time in that school
        of longing and resistance, sometime citizen

of the knot I threaded nights on my way anywhere,
 under what the builders have chopped
  to a broken arm of a tree.

Nearly everything we said beneath it
 concerned our endless desires,
  the thing that doth shine and so torment us,

our coins passed from hand to hand
 until their inscriptions all but wore away.
  Those old longings—at least

we said them to each other. *We are*
 of interest to one another, are we not?
  The evangelical woman, she of the superb hat,

will she look down from that glassy paradise
 and find me of interest, or the men and women
  who unroll blankets over flattened cardboard

under Barney's stainless awning,
 its steel-cloud sheen? They sleep
  and dream before a chamber

gleaming with refusal all night,
 inviting no one in, sealed plate glass
  displaying—ready?—necklaces,

shown on featureless, streamlined busts
 under relentless halogen
  the better to foreground *shine.*

Three yards away, tulips fenced
 in iron spear-tips wrap wings
  around their furnace flames,

heat drawn up from the center
 of the earth: a strength never bridled yet.
  Even the mutilated tree aura'd

in a froth of green: no intention to quit,
 none whatsoever. The tower's blank surface
  offers fewer chances to engage,

an old church's ramshackle intimacy
    shrinks beneath what we all see coming:
        a seamless façade interested only in itself,

hulking over the red brick it doesn't crush
    because—why should it? The air rights
        are for sale. Fit yourself around

whatever it is you want, pay them
    some fraction—enormous, in their eyes,
        but nothing to the unreal numbers

you'll accrue. Build, and keep on display
    what you swallowed to erect this chilly
        Babel tower on my block.

I'm all judgment, I know; the Congregation
    won't regret the sale of light and air,
        and those who sleep on Seventh Avenue,

their midnights raked by precious glitter—
    on the space between their skulls
        and the empyrean, no one puts a price.

The new tower's a glacial expanse.
    The tulips ember in their spiky bed.
        We dwell down here in shadow and in spring.

From the Poet

Those who "handle money" on a larger scale don't handle it at all. For decades the deregulation of financial practice, and the concomitant separation of money from anything it represents, even from the status of object in itself, has multiplied with astonishing speed. I suspect I wouldn't think about this odd phantom economy as much if I didn't live in a place where people make unthinkable fortunes moving numbers around in arcanely coded operations.

When I bought my place in Chelsea, in 2001, the neighborhood had been colonized by gay men, but the end of that phase was in the air. The gay-themed businesses on 8th Avenue were starting to wink out, and, just behind them, the small, individually owned businesses were going, too. Today, the sleekly remodeled, newly vacant marble husk of Barney's occupies one corner of my block. Toward the other end, a new condominium tower looms over the nineteenth-century French Evangelical Church, fourteen stories of bluestone, steel, and glass, still unfinished.

It seems naïve to complain about gentrification in Manhattan, the center of a city that's been tearing itself down, rebuilding itself since its beginning. City of no limits, city of vaulting ambitions. I couldn't begin to count how much has disappeared in the years I've lived here, the comfortable cafés and modestly priced restaurants, many bookstores, at least two of my old gyms, the basement 12-step meeting spaces, a host of faces. People who welcomed me in that impersonal way that city people come to recognize each other, to create from the random and incidental a fabric of urban life.

Then new faces appear. In an odd triangular pocket formed by plywood walls surrounding the base of that new condo tower, a young man lives, at least at night, when his sleeping form is often hidden under a pile of brightly colored blankets. Or there's Sills, a woman who spends many days on a low, apparently unused set of stairs between two furniture stores just now gone out of business. She collects a little money for food, mostly from regulars, I think.

The Barney's people used to trouble me the most. They'd camp on Seventh Avenue, under the cloud-colored awning of brushed stainless steel, seeking shelter from rain or snow. They spread layers of cardboard at the base of the big display windows and slept with their heads at the driest spot, their heads often touching the glass, so that the homeless were literally sleeping against cases of jewels or fantastically expensive shoes.

Strangely ironic, now that Barney's has gone under and glows emptily all night, stripped of everything but a few fixtures and its lavish marble floors. In the future, it may seem that the last two decades were the easier times, a quieter prelude to the twenty-first century's real arrival, when the ravaging consequences of greed became undeniably clear: nearly 40 million on unemployment, this city for months the global epicenter of a raging pandemic, the poor and hungry on these streets increasingly desperate, the police seemingly under no one's control.

Is every human era one of unbridled appetite? If the poet lives face to face with the relentless progress of appetite—his own and others—what is the work of poetry?

Jane Hirshfield

Jane Hirshfield has published nine collections of poetry, most
recently *Ledger* (Knopf, 2020), and two books of essays, including
Ten Windows: How Great Poems Transform the World (Knopf, 2015).
Hirshfield's honors include fellowships from the Guggenheim and
Rockefeller foundations, the NEA, and the Academy of American Poets,
and her work appears in ten editions of *The Best American Poetry*. In 2012,
she was elected a chancellor of the Academy of American Poets. In 2019,
she was elected into the American Academy of Arts & Sciences.

～ In My Wallet I Carry a Card

In my wallet I carry a card
which declares I have the power to marry.

In my wallet I carry a card
which declares I may drive.

In my wallet I carry a card
that says to a merchant I may be trusted to pay her.

In my wallet I carry a card
that states I can borrow a book in the town where I live.

In my hand I carry a card.
Its lines declare I am cardless, carless,
stateless, and have no money.

It is buoyant and edgeless.
It names me one of the Order of All Who Will Die.

～ My Luck

My luck
lay in the road
copper side up
and copper side down
It shone
I passed it by
I turned around
I picked it up
I shook
my beggar's cup
quite full
I left it there
to be refound
I bent down and
I unbent up
copper side down
copper side up

between the air
and ground
left there picked up
My luck

∼ Three-Legged Blues

Always you were given
one too many, one too few.
What almost happens, doesn't.
What might be lost, you'll lose.
The crows will eat your garden.
Weeds will get what's left.
Your cats will be three-legged,
your house's mice be blessed.
One friend will take your husband,
another wear your dress.
No, it isn't what you wanted.
It isn't what you'd choose.
Your floors have always slanted.
Your roof has paid its dues.
Life delivered you a present—
a too-small pair of shoes.
What almost happened, won't now.
What can be lost, you'll lose.

From the Poet

In the 1925 edition of *Roget's Thesaurus*, the first listing for "capital" appears, unsurprisingly, under the category of "money." Among the list of synonyms, not very far down: "rhino, blunt, dust, mopus, tin, salt, chink." Higher up: "sinews of war," "almighty dollar," "needful." Lower: "wampum," "lac of rupees," "plum." The word's second-place index listing sends the reader to "wealth." There you can find among its companion concepts: "*El Dorado*," "Pactolus," "Golconda," "Potosi"; also the more easily comprehended but equally culturally dependent "alimony" and "dowry."

The Pactolus, further research reveals, is a Turkish river near the Aegean coast. Its sediments contain electrum, a naturally occurring alloy of silver and gold. Electrum from the Pactolus underlay the economy of the ancient state of Lydia, the first Western imperium to issue coins and open shops; when mixed—debased—with copper, it was known as "green gold." According to myth, King Midas first deposited the riverbed's stores of precious metals when he washed in the Pactolus to undo his curse. King Croesus's legendary riches, according to Herodotus, were drawn from its waters. A photograph shows a pretty, greenish river passing between scenic white rocks.

In the midst of these readings, I find myself pausing to eat a small, flat peach of perfect color and ripeness. Gone in a few quick bites, in what is likely the last possible hour it would be good.

Though a peach's ripeness will always elude "Possessive Relations"—the larger category in which all words related to capital appear—I take my pencil and add to the *Thesaurus*: "peach." Surely no less incomprehensible to someone in the future than "rhino," "blunt," and "dust" are now to me. I write it not next to "plum," but where there's a bit of extra space: right after the entry "loaves and fishes," at the end of a list that begins "pelf," "Mammon," "lucre," "filthy lucre."

The presence of plum is explained—somewhat—in an online dictionary of slang: *A desirable thing. A raisin, when used in a pudding or cake. (pejorative) A fool, idiot. (slang, usually in plural) A testicle. The edible, fleshy stone fruit of Prunus mume, an Asian fruit more closely related to the apricot than the plum, usually consumed pickled, dried, or as a juice or wine; ume.* I am oddly delighted to find that last, Japanese word in the entry.

A writer's capital is language, which, it seems, is as slippery as any other kind of wealth, as potentially cursed if held without nuance, as transient, as bluntly and inextricably subjective. A briefly borrowed inheritance; a street-found penny. In another ninety years, I can't help but wonder, will "penny" be a word so unfamiliar it too will need looking up, another mopus? Yet to be penniless will be just as painful when named in some other way.

Dorianne Laux

Pulitzer Prize finalist Dorianne Laux's most recent collections
are *Only As the Day Is Long: New and Selected* (W. W. Norton, 2019),
The Book of Men (W. W. Norton, 2012), winner of the Paterson Poetry Prize,
and *Facts about the Moon* (W. W. Norton, 2007), winner of the Oregon
Book Award. She teaches poetry in the MFA program at North Carolina
State University and is founding faculty at Pacific University's low
residency Master of Fine Arts in Writing program.

∽ Waitress

When I was young and had to rise at 5 AM
I did not look at the lamplight slicing
through the blinds and say: Once again
I have survived the night. I did not raise
my two hands to my face and whisper:
This is the miracle of my flesh. I walked
toward the cold water waiting to be released
and turned the tap so I could listen to it
thrash through the rusted pipes.
I cupped my palms and thought of nothing.

I dressed in my blue uniform and went to work.
I served the public, looked down on its
balding skulls, the knitted shawls draped
over its cancerous shoulders, and took its orders,
wrote *up* or *easy* or *scrambled* or *poached*
in the yellow pads' margins and stabbed it through
the tip of the fry cook's deadly planchette.

Those days I barely had a pulse. The manager
had vodka for breakfast, the busboys hid behind
the bleach boxes from the immigration cops,
and the head waitress took ten percent
of our tips and stuffed them in her pocket
with her cigarettes and lipstick. My feet
hurt. I balanced the meatloaf-laden trays.
Even the tips of my fingers ached.

I thought of nothing except sleep, a T.V. set's
flickering cathode gleam washing over me,
baptizing my greasy body in its watery light.
And money, slipping the tassel of my coin purse
aside, opening the silver clasp, staring deep
into that dark sacrificial abyss.

What can I say about that time, those years
I leaned over the rickety balcony on my break
smoking my last saved butt?

It was sheer bad luck when I picked up
the glass coffee pot and spun around
to pour another cup. All I could think
as it shattered was how it was the same size
and shape as the customer's head. And this is why
I don't believe in accidents, the grainy dregs
running like sludge down his thin tie
and pinstripe shirt like they were channels
riven for just this purpose.

It wasn't my fault. I know that. But what, really,
was the hurry? I dabbed at his belly with a napkin.
He didn't have a cut on him (physics) and only
his earlobe was burned. But my last day there
was the first day I looked up as I walked, the trees
shimmering green lanterns under the Prussian blue
particulate sky, sun streaming between my fingers
as I waved at the bus, running, breathing hard, thinking:
This is the grand phenomenon of my body. This thirst
is mine. This is my one and only life.

∽ The Tooth Fairy

They brushed a quarter with glue
and glitter, slipped in on bare
feet, and without waking me,
painted rows of delicate gold
footprints on my sheets with a love
so quiet, I still can't hear it.

My mother must have been
a beauty then, sitting
at the kitchen table with him,
a warm breeze lifting her
embroidered curtains, waiting
for me to fall asleep.

It's harder to believe
the years that followed, the palms

curled into fists, a floor
of broken dishes, her chain-smoking
through long silences, him
punching holes in his walls.

I can still remember her print
dresses, his checkered taxi, the day
I found her in the closet
with a paring knife, the night
he kicked my sister in the ribs.

He lives alone in Oregon now, dying
slowly of a rare disease.
His face stippled gray, his ankles
clotted beneath wool socks.

She's a nurse on the graveyard shift.
Comes home mornings and calls me.
Drinks her dark beer and goes to bed.

And I still wonder how they did it, slipped
that quarter under my pillow, made those
perfect footprints . . .

Whenever I visit her, I ask again.
"I don't know," she says, rocking, closing
her eyes. "We were as surprised as you."

From the Poet

"The Tooth Fairy" is a true story, one that always haunted me when re-
membered in tandem with the violence, abuse, and mental illness that
existed in my family. No mother and father start out thinking that they
will hurt each other or their children. They begin like all couples, with a
sense of innocence and hope for the future. In that respect, the poem is an
echoed response to Sharon Olds's poem "I Go Back to May, 1937." Olds
gave me the courage to go back myself and view with dispassion the young
couple that became my parents, to see who they were before they became
who they would be.

Most of my life I worked as a waitress, and back then, waitresses lived
on their tips. Our paychecks were small, not enough to cover rent, gas and

electric, phone, food and clothing. Tips took up the slack. Even so, there were many end-of-the-months we would eat tortillas and cheese, or macaroni and cheese, or grilled cheese sandwiches. To make great tips, one had to be either a good waitress or a good talker or beautiful. I wasn't any of those things, and so I made only decent tips, but envied those who did better. We knew who did well and who didn't because it was a ritual to stand around at the end of a shift and count tips out. On the other hand, if anyone was in trouble or needed something, we all chipped in to help—with rent, food, doctor's bills, a baby shower, birthday and holiday gifts. No one ever wanted for anything in a family of waitresses.

Years later, when I was, unaccountably, a creative writing professor on sabbatical in Italy, I found in my bedside drawer the only book in English in the whole city: a copy of Dostoyevsky's first novel, *Poor Folk*. What struck me was the way the characters shared what little they had. If someone got a windfall of some kind—a sack of potatoes or rice, an extra loaf of bread, a piece of fruit, a bolt of fabric, a holiday box of chocolates or a cake from a relative—they shared it, or they contrived to seek out the poorest among them to offer it up. The goods and money went around and around the poverty-stricken neighborhood so that no one went hungry or without. The novel reminded me that those who have the least give the most because they know what it's like to have nothing. Even now, in the midst of the COVID-19 pandemic, we see the same phenomenon in people making masks, supporting their local hospitals, and sharing goods and food. During tough times, humanity shines through.

Afaa Michael Weaver

The son of a sharecropper, Afaa Michael Weaver is the author of fifteen books of poems, most recently *Spirit Boxing* (University of Pittsburgh Press, 2017). His earlier collections include *The Government of Nature* (University of Pittsburgh Press, 2013), winner of the 2014 Kingsley Tufts Award, and *City of Eternal Spring* (University of Pittsburgh Press, 2014), winner of the 2015 Phillis Wheatley Book Award. Weaver's honors include the May Sarton Award, a Pew Fellowship, a Fulbright scholarship, and the Gold Friendship Medal from the Beijing Writers' Association.

∽ Ivory Soap, a Whiteness

In the hot houses the soap waits
in innocence, purely white, soft, hard,

cut up from the long tubes of ooze
from the vats where men sweat, knobs

for the making of the clean, washing
the souls like the Akan priests, sage work,

Adams letting the Eves fall from them,
Eves gathering dust to make the Adams,

all histories writ and rewritten anew,
again and again, until the company is awash

in profit hallelujahs. I open the door,
let the steam of Ivory soap whiteness

fill me and take the trays to Arty, whose
work is to feed the bars to the machine,

its stamps of logos, guarantees of purity
embossed in the writing, the bosses of America's

dirt watching to see that the machines
do not rest from the perfect form of bars

of soap sliding down the rubber belts,
under the spray of salty water, into the metal

stamp plates, the wrappers with hot sealers
for paper, Arty, an Aikido master of the line,

stopping to tell me the details of Russia
from his last summer vacation, to ask

my opinion on Islam, the Arab slave trade,
the business of taking masters' names,

the thump and slide of the motor pulling
the rubber belt, the bars of Ivory a broken

whiteness marching out to stores to wash
away the sluggish shame of being dirty,

cash registers counting the money we make
for masters who sit in invisible places,

designing our wages, what wages can buy,
while men like my father, black and white,

wash bodies aching with layers of sweat
from mills and the holds of ships filthy

` with what it takes to make a life in a nation
obese with forgetting, hungry for what is new.

⌒ A Postscript to Giant

In the backseat of that yellow Buick he bought
working at the cotton mill, at the Drive-In
under the full moon, her mama and daddy gone
down to Macon to see Aunt Sally, nothing
to hold them back from pulling at each other
until before the moon could say how sprite it was
they were pulled on top of each other, flipping
open the door to consequences. He been working
twice as hard ever since. That movie was *Giant*,
don't they remember? Every time he asks her,
they get older in the gray hobbling along, alone.

Down by that creek on his daddy's first place
there was a frog that used to croak out like it knew
what would happen if he messed with her. Kiss Clara,
won't nothing ever be clear again, pull on her lips
as long as you want you'll be pulling lines to move
long rails of steel in place on construction sites,
worlds for other men, filling their bank accounts.

            The frog croaked to dumb ears
when they eased into each other, forgetting all about
James Dean covered with black crude trying to seduce
the one beauty, Elizabeth Taylor, while the beauty
of a naked innocence dies, a debt sealed by paper.

∽ Repack Room

A coffee pot, chairs for tired joints, the morning paper,
our warehouse was a kinder place to men in their late years,
old timers who hobbled from leg to leg on sore knees
that had climbed up onto forklifts for forty years, had fallen,
slipped and fell on the cement floor when it took on ice
in winter and the galvanized walls made winter sharper
when we forgot our thermals or forgot we were getting
too old to be without them. This was the company's
blind eye turned to men who could not still keep up
with production lines and quotas for loading trucks,
men who had fought in WWII and Korea, who had
loaded shells on giant anti-aircraft guns on ships at sea,
defending home and coming home to make what was
a fortune to the poor and pennies to the rich. One sore
knee to the other, one strained back to the other, one
set of clogged and swollen arteries to another, trading
pictures of their grandchildren, planning trips to Mexico,
in the evening of a life of duty, and now in my evening
I think of duty, of who owns us and what gifts we give
now that I am old enough for the repack room, the slow
job of salvaging good bars of soap from busted boxes,
the spirit of my old worker sitting in an office with books.

From the Poet

In *The Life of Poetry*, Muriel Rukeyser suggests that poetry in American culture has to struggle against the distractions of a consumer economy. There are too many things that keep us from having intimate moments with poetry. I would not disagree with that, but I would like to go inside the production of distractions, to reflect for a moment on what it was like to work at my development as a poet while also working in factories in my native Baltimore. That time was a constant battle against the mindlessness of the environment. I worked for Bethlehem Steel and for Procter & Gamble—the company that launched soap operas, a mother lode of distractions and, some might argue, of mindlessness.

Capital is centuries old, but the set of circumstances that created the enormous machine that produces the complexity, diversity, and overabundance of commodities that we have now did not arise, as we know, until the unfolding of European colonialism. In the 1890s the Bethlehem Steel plant in Sparrows Point, Maryland, became the largest mass production facility in the world. It is just outside Baltimore proper, and as a child, I watched my father leave the house to go to work at "The Point." He was a model of dignity, and I did not know where he headed each day until I took my first factory job there in the spring of 1970, my books in hand, wrapped in brown paper from old lunch bags. I took whatever time and quiet space I could find to read and write safely. Machinery weighing hundreds of tons swirled and spun around me. I set out to make of myself something the system had not intended, a poet.

Six months into the year, I went into the military for basic training, where I learned other ways of being a machine. I continued my adversarial relationship with the system by writing poems, sometimes love poems I sold to other soldiers. For the next fourteen years, I made soap at Proctor & Gamble, still shaping myself against a system that all too easily could grind your imagination and freedom of headspace into dust. When I left P&G after receiving a $20,000 fellowship from the National Endowment for the Arts, the company offered my coworkers an early retirement package— including $20,000. It felt as if they were trying to devalue my accomplishment. I could have seen it as my having inspired the liberation of a few, were it not for the fact that the company, one of the few to pay dividends during the Great Depression, was looking for ways to reduce expenditures and increase profits.

Working as I did meant that I had jobs, jobs that family and friends described as "good." In the greater mind of compassion, work is about creating gainful and rewarding means of earning a living and sharing wealth. But capitalism feeds on greed; capital is invested so that greater capital can be gained. The world is filled with factories, and I wonder what we have done to ourselves. However, I am a firm believer in gratitude. I invested the capital of my creativity and my experience—which has been painful at times—into the realization of my soul.

Kathleen Hellen

Born in Tokyo and half Japanese, Kathleen Hellen is the author of
The Only Country Was the Color of My Skin (Saddle Road Press, 2018),
Umberto's Night (Washington Writers Publishing House, 2012), and two
chapbooks. Her poems have been awarded the Washington Writers' Poetry
Prize, the Thomas Merton Prize, and prizes from the *H.O.W. Journal* and
Washington Square Review. She has won grants from the Maryland State
Arts Council and the Baltimore Office of Promotion & the Arts.

∾ The Dirty Work of Quarters

"I tried to kill myself," the drunk insists. Grins gin. A six-day binge.
You look away but he persists. Your heart's a small balloon you think
feels punctured. "Spare a dollar? A lousy quarter?"

Luminous in headlights, flailing in her cardboard rant at traffic, she's
a pressure in your chest against the cage of your intention. A headline's
intersection. *Murders Up—From the Previous Quarter.*

Tapping at the glass, a squeegee in his hand, he fingerprints the windshield
of your consciousness. You cushion in the console a roll of metered feed.
Weigh the need. An embarrassment of quarters.

What she stuffs into the pockets of her cargo: free pencils. Free candy. Free
magnets. She reads *People.* Where does she sleep when the reading room
closes? Where's the weekend's safe quarter?

You see him in periphery, filling in the blanks—*name, SSN.* The last
address the shelter. His disease? The way it hurts to be: Asthmatic.
    Diabetic.
HIV-positive. $600M in healthcare earnings, quartered.

Cold anniversary. I peer into rooms where the chairs were removed. The
    table,
sofa, consigned. Where curtains once fluttered, where photographs
    welcomed
the stairs. Derived. Sub-prime. The mortgaged quarters.

∾ How Light Bends at the Exxon

Behind the bullet-glass, he waves, as I wave back.
"Nice day," he says, as if he means the weather.
As if the sympathies of heat could teach us better:
gallons/dollars/cents. Numbers in their lotteries of
cause/effect. $3.99—no more or less deterrent than
a nuclear solution. The sun is shifting closer.
Pansies in the pot light up like flares in distant places.
I lift the lever. Nozzle fitted, air expands. The light
reflected bends. A hundred-thousand casualties of

earth and men. The means like ends. Like shifting
sands under the traffic's caravan. I start the engine.

↶ The Erotic Has No Use

Morning fog hid the bottom, the sun was coming up.
What was it passed between us? A god with wings?
A silver token in a flip
unraveled from the crop of cotton in his pocket—

a mercury as liquid as the dreams that I would dream, later.

Turning it over. My head a gang of snakes. The sky
a bowl, a water pot, the rain holding out.

I'd been all night crying.
His rig was hired, idling.
What was it this man offered?
A coin in cardboard. Mounted.
A memory of kindness.

The dime his dying father passed him, the last of its kind
before Roosevelt died. What if the earth were not a rock
held up by other rocks?

I hug myself as if I could contain it. Sky rushed pink.
The swollen worms hermaphroditic, coiling.
From the west, the smell of money.
The possibility of some exchange.

From the Poet

When I was seven or eight, my sister and I were each appointed a small
patch on which to grow a garden. For this happy project, I had selected
bachelor buttons, the petals ravishingly blue, vivifying, the frilly, showy
flowers worn in the lapels of suitors in days past—hence the name. They
grew wild in sunlit stretches, which further appealed to my instincts, and I
couldn't wait to plant the seeds.

I watered and weeded. I tended the sprigs. My sister, on the other hand,
planted lettuce. When the gardens sprouted, revealing what each of us

had selected, my father turned to me, his disappointment unequivocal. "You can't make soup out of roses," he said.

My father believed that work had value only as exchange—a day's work for a day's pay. For him, this garden had no value other than the practical, and my choice to plant these bright-blue blooms instead of something "useful" heralded for me a life of insecurity and hardship. How many times had I heard the stories? How he'd grown up suffering shoes that didn't fit. The bread lines. How he'd stood outside the storefront at Odelli's, his mouth watering, imagining the sweetness in the bins. "You're always going the wrong way," he said.

And yet, decades later, when he was sick, in hospice, among his valuables— the summaries and bank accounts, the deed, the trust—was a poem I'd titled "Rice." This poem, this product made of memory and hours in re- vision, hadn't earned a cent in publication, but I'd offered it as a gift. I could only guess why he'd kept it—what usefulness it might have had (outside my therapy in writing it), what it meant—this "Rosebud" among his valu- ables. Did it remind him of how he'd taught me once to cook a pot of rice? Did it validate his usefulness to me, aside from the accident of fathering?

Like love, like forgiveness—a poem exists outside the function of exchange.

Dana Gioia

Former California Poet Laureate and Chairman of the
National Endowment for the Arts, Dana Gioia has published five
full-length collections of verse, most recently *99 Poems: New & Selected*
(Graywolf, 2016), which won the Poets' Prize as the best new book of the
year. His third collection, *Interrogations at Noon* (Graywolf, 2001), was
awarded the American Book Award. For fifteen years, he worked as a
businessman before quitting at forty-one to become a full-time writer.

◡ Money

> Money is a kind of poetry.
>
> —Wallace Stevens

Money, the long green,
cash, stash, rhino, jack
or just plain dough.

Chock it up, fork it over,
shell it out. Watch it
burn holes through pockets.

To be made of it! To have it
to burn! Greenbacks, double eagles,
megabucks and Ginnie Maes.

It greases the palm, feathers a nest,
holds heads above water,
makes both ends meet.

Money breeds money.
Gathering interest, compounding daily.
Always in circulation.

Money. You don't know where it's been,
but you put it where your mouth is.
And it talks.

◡ Shopping

I enter the temple of my people but do not pray.
I pass the altars of the gods but do not kneel
Or offer sacrifices proper to the season.

Strolling the hushed aisles of the department store,
I see visions shining under glass,
Divinities of leather, gold, and porcelain,
Shrines of cut crystal, stainless steel, and silicon.

But I wander the arcades of abundance,
Empty of desire, no credit to my people,
Envying the acolytes their passionate faith.

Blessed are the acquisitive,
For theirs is the kingdom of commerce.

Redeem me, gods of the mall and marketplace.
Mercury, protector of cell phones and fax machines,
Venus, patroness of bath and bedroom chains,
Tantalus, guardian of the food court.

Beguile me with the aromas of coffee, musk, and cinnamon.
Surround me with delicately colored soaps and moisturizing creams.
Comfort me with posters of children with perfect smiles
And pouting teenage models clad in lingerie.
I am not made of stone.

Show me satins, linen, crêpe de chine, and silk,
Heaped like cumuli in the morning sky,
As if all caravans and argosies ended in this parking lot
To fill these stockrooms and loading docks.

Sing me the hymns of no cash down and the installment plan,
Of custom fit, remote control, and priced to move.
Whisper the blessing of Egyptian cotton, polyester, and cashmere.
Tell me in what department my desire shall be found.

Because I would buy happiness if I could find it,
Spend all that I possessed or could borrow.
But what can I bring you from these sad emporia?
Where in this splendid clutter
Shall I discover the one true thing?

Nothing to carry, I should stroll easily
Among the crowded countertops and eager cashiers,
Bypassing the sullen lines and footsore customers,
Spending only my time, discounting all I see.

Instead I look for you among the pressing crowds,
But they know nothing of you, turning away,
Carrying their brightly packaged burdens.
There is no angel among the vending stalls and signage.

Where are you, my fugitive? Without you
There is nothing but the getting and the spending
Of things that have a price.

Why else have I stalked the leased arcades
Searching the kiosks and the cash machines?

Where are you, my errant soul and innermost companion?
Are you outside amid the potted palm trees,
Bumming a cigarette or joking with the guards,
Or are you wandering the parking lot
Lost among the rows of Subarus and Audis?

Or is it you I catch a sudden glimpse of
Smiling behind the greasy window of the bus
As it disappears into the evening rush?

From the Poet

Some readers may object to poems about money or a shopping mall—or
at least to mall or money poems that don't contain fiery denunciations of
capitalism, the monetary system, or consumer culture. These folks would
have a point. We live in a society excessively fixated on wealth and material
acquisition. A culture in which value is measured in monetary terms is a
culture without values.

Poems, however, are not editorials. The poems I like best tend to pro-
voke questions rather than provide answers. One of the purposes of poetry,
it seems to me, is to visit the complicated places in which we really live—for
better or for worse—and redeem them for the imagination. These two
poems both attempt what W. H. Auden once described as the clear expres-
sion of mixed feelings.

Money is the only dirty subject left in poetry. My first poem—quite
deliberately—has no single point of view. It cites and juxtaposes everyday
metaphors that Americans use to describe money. The subject of every line
is the same. The revelations are in the images and associations. "Money"
lets the American language speak for itself. Every reader will hear the poem
in slightly different ways—some of them contradictory, all of them true.

"Shopping" explores the temples of our consumer culture—the shop-
ping mall. What forces draw people to these crowded retail plazas and
gallerias? What are they searching for? I try to reflect both the allure and
the repulsion I feel. It is the poet's task to search for the sacred hidden in
the profane. I hope my susceptible pilgrim finds a *soupçon* of grace in his
rambling journey through the marketplace. As J. R. R. Tolkien once said,
"Not all who wander are lost."

John Bradley

John Bradley is the author of ten books of poetry and prose,
most recently *Everything in Motion, Everything at Rest* (Dos Madres, 2020).
A recipient of two National Endowment for the Arts fellowships,
he frequently reviews books of poetry for *Rain Taxi*.

◠ What Money Can Buy

I.

She offered to kiss me right there. Vicki.
On the Meadowlark Lane School playground.

First grade recess. For a quarter. I pondered the offer.
Twenty-five cents. For a kiss. From Vickie.

I reached into my pocket, felt the quarter. She waited.
No one in the playground looking in our direction.

I handed her the quarter. She pursed her lips,
I closed my eyes and claimed the purchased kiss.

First: *I paid a quarter. For this?* And then:
I paid only a quarter. For this.

2.

Each week, I stacked them—rows of quarters
on the glass counter for Mr. Walters to count.

Quarters surrendered by customers of the *Long Island Press*
for the pleasure of finding a newspaper at their doorstep

each day. Mr. Walters scooped the change into his hand
and then counted out the weightless greenbacks.

One of those I handed back for a Forever Yours
and the latest Batman comic book. Those quarters

he gave me for change: hadn't they just been
in the rows piled across the glass counter?

3.

The notice on the job board called for movers. The hardest part
would be arriving at the student center parking lot at exactly

five a.m. But I needed the job. In the car, I nodded off on the drive
into the mountains to Fairplay. As we pulled into the long driveway

to the ranch buildings, the landlord said, *I'm evicting the tenants.*
Don't talk to them. If you see one of them pull a gun, tell me,

and I'll call the sheriff. I hauled their belongings—clothes,
silverware, buckets of rusted bolts—with the other hired hands,

and dumped it all along the side of the road, as if it were trash.
When the landlord wasn't in sight, I quietly apologized

to the woman—*We didn't know we'd be evicting someone.*
But the worst part, the part I wish were a lie—I went back

there, to Fairplay, to work the next day.

ᷗ As Blood Is the Fruit of the Heart

As she was removing the shoplifting device from the white shirt
As was required of her by the motion and mechanics of her job
As the machine used to remove the device caught her finger
As she knew her finger would bleed even before it bled
As she didn't want blood upon the front of the new white shirt
As she was holding a Band-Aid in her other hand to keep it ready
As a long line of customers armed with clothing formed behind me
As she paged Jason or Jennifer to come to the front desk now please
As there can be no job without a Job no Job without a job
As I didn't want to call attention to her act of inattention
As I didn't want to insult the blood on the front of the white shirt
As blood adores compliments but is easily bruised
As it was her blood and not the store's or her supervisor's
As she explained how some shoppers remove shoplifting devices
As desire lurks in the blood no matter your zip code
As I listened while she complained which made me complicit
As I was a fellow bearer and lifetime spiller of that same fluid
As I could always take the shirt back when it wasn't her shift
As I didn't want her to be penalized for the action of her blood
As no one should have to apologize for the suction of a job
As ketchup or wine or olive oil would one day claim the shirt
As I left the store with the damp blotch on the shirt's whiteness
As the shoplifting scanner by the front door did not detect fresh blood
As blood contains beauty in movement but not beauty in stillness
As I washed the shirt relentlessly with cold water and soap once home
As blood calls for kindness even as it calls for erasure

As I couldn't bear to wear a bloodstained shirt to the wedding
As I knew my wife would see the blotch even before she saw the shirt
As I removed from the shirt the worker and the worker's error
As white eventually yellows even as we continue to call it white
As there is a drop of blood in our every article of clothing
As you cannot spot the blood on the shirt unless you know where to
    imagine it
As there can be no ecstasy no sorrow without blood

From the Poet

My introduction to money—mainly quarters—came from my job as a paper-
boy in Lynbrook, New York. I was a carrier for the *Long Island Press*, delivering
the paper to sixty-one customers every day of the week, collecting money
from them each Friday, and paying the route manager each Saturday. As
"What Money Can Buy" describes, I went each Saturday to the Lynbrook
drugstore, which no longer sold drugs but still had a soda fountain. I stacked
my quarters for Mr. Walters and, in exchange, received fresh dollar bills to
pay the manager Mr. Foley what I owed for the week's papers.

In a green route book, I listed who owed and how much. Some folks
would be hard to find—it might take me four or more weeks to collect from
them. Some folks always gave me a tip; some never did. Soon I had money
of my own to spend. This was a big decision. What did I want? A transistor
radio would let me listen to music, even in bed on summer nights when it
was too hot to sleep. I bought a small Sony, one of the best "toys" I ever had.
Later, when I was in high school, I bought a typewriter, a turquoise portable
Olivetti. Though I thought I bought it for school papers, I soon discovered
I wanted to be a writer—whatever that meant—and I began to bang out
poems, godawful ones.

But there was much more to learn about money and employment. The
event described in "As Blood Is the Fruit of the Heart" happened at a T. J.
Maxx, here in DeKalb, Illinois. It felt like a dream. The cashier's blood on
my white shirt, despite many scrubbings and washings, never completely
went away.

I suppose I could have taken the shirt back to the store, but I needed a
white shirt that weekend for a wedding. (Or was it a funeral?) And it felt
fitting that the person who injured herself while selling me that shirt should
leave her signature on it. I doubt that those in corporate offices have any

idea what work is like for the invisible figures who labor in their stores. The cuts and bruises on the hand. The insults from impatient customers. Those who never speak to them at all, carrying on conversation on the cell phone. Above all, the shitty pay that's impossible to live on. And now, with the pandemic, we rely even more on workers like this clerk, who risk their lives for us every day, with little reward or respect. (Yes, I'm talking to you, Mr. Bezos.) It still confounds me what we do, what we endure for money.

Edward Hirsch

Edward Hirsch, a MacArthur Fellow, has published
ten books of poems, most recently *Stranger by Night* (2020) and
The Living Fire: New and Selected Poems (2010), both from Knopf.
He has also published five prose books, among them *A Poet's Glossary*
(Houghton Mifflin Harcourt, 2014) and *How to Read a Poem and Fall in
Love with Poetry* (Harcourt Brace, 1999), a national bestseller. He
started out working summer jobs as a bus boy, a soda fountain jerk,
a garbage man, and a factory worker. He's currently president of
the John Simon Guggenheim Memorial Foundation.

∾ Mergers and Acquisitions

Beyond junk bonds and oil spills,
beyond the collapse of Savings and Loans,
beyond liquidations and options on futures,
beyond basket trading and expanding foreign markets,
the Dow Jones Industrial Average, the Standard
& Poor's stock index, mutual funds, commodities,
beyond the rising tide of debits and credits,
opinion polls, falling currencies, the signs
for L.A. Gear and Coca-Cola Classic,
the signs for U.S. Steel and General Motors,
hi-grade copper, municipal bonds, domestic sugar,
beyond fax it and collateral buildups,
beyond mergers and acquisitions, leveraged buyouts,
hostile takeovers, beyond the official policy
on inflation and the consensus on happiness,
beyond the national trends in buying and selling,
getting and spending, the market stalled
and the cost passed on to consumers,
beyond the statistical charts on prices,
there is something else that drives us, some
rage or hunger, some absence smoldering
like a childhood fever vaguely remembered
or half-perceived, some unprotected desire,
greed that is both wound and knife,
a failed grief, a lost radiance.

∾ Cold Calls

If you had watched my father,
who had been peddling boxes for 50 years,
working the phones again at a common desk,

if you had listened to him sweet-talking
the newly minted Assistant Buyer at Seagram's

and swearing a little under his breath,

if you had sweated with him on the docks
of a medical supply company
and heard him boasting, as I did,
that he had to kiss some strange asses,

if you had seen him dying out there,

then you would understand why I stood
at his grave on those wintry afternoons
and stared at the bare muddy trees

and raved in silence to no one,
to his name carved into a granite slab . . .

Cold calls, dead accounts.

∿ Liberty Brass

I was sitting across from the rotating sign
For the Liberty Brass Turning Company

Automatic Screw Machine Products

And brooding about our fathers
Always on the make to make more money

Screw Machine Products Automatic

Tender wounded brassy unsystematic
Free American men obsessing about margins

Machine Products Automatic Screw

Selling every day of their God-damned lives
To some Liberty Brass Turning Company

Products Automatic Screw Machine

Until they were screwed into boxes
And planted in plots paid and unpaid

Automatic Screw Machine Products

∾ Second-Story Warehouse
Summer 1966

Come with me to the second-story warehouse
   where I filled orders for the factory downstairs,
and commanded the freight elevator, and read
   high in the air on a floating carpet of boxes.

I could touch the damp pipes in the ceiling
   and smell the rust. I could look over
the Puerto Rican workers in the parking lot,
   smoking and laughing and kidding around

in Spanish during their break, especially Julia,
   who bit my lower lip until it bruised and bled,
and taught me to roll cigarettes in another language,
   and called me her virgin boy from the suburbs.

All summer I read Neruda's *Canto General*
   and took lessons from Juan, who trained me
to accept orders with dignity—*dignidad*—
   and never take any shit from the foreman.

He showed off the iron plate in his skull
   from a bar fight with a drunken supervisor,
while the phone blinked endlessly from Shipping
   & Handling, and light glinted off the forklift.

I felt like a piece of wavy, fluted paper
   trapped between two sheets of linerboard
in the single wall, double-faced boxes
   we lifted and cursed, sweated and stacked

on top of heavy wooden skids. I dreaded
   the large, unwieldy industrial A-flutes
and the 565 stock cartons that we carried
   in bundles through the dusty aisles

while downstairs a line of blue collars fed
   slotting, gluing, and stitching machines.
Juan taught me about mailers and multidepths
   and praised the torrential rains of childhood,

the oysters that hid in the bloody coral,
   their pearls shimmering in the twisted rock,
green stones polished by furious storms
   and coconut palms waving in the twilight.

He praised the sun that floats over the island
   like a bell ringed with fire, or a sea rose,
and the secret torch that forever burns
   inside us, a beacon no one can touch.

Come with me to the second-story warehouse
   where I learned the difference between
RSC, FOL, die-cuts, and five-panel folders,
   and saw the iron shine inside a skull.

Every day at precisely three in the afternoon
   we delivered our orders to the loading dock.
We may go down dusty and tired, Juan said,
   but we come back smelling like the sea.

From the Poet

Part of the work of poetry is to take up the poetry of work. It's not all about love, death, and the changing of the seasons. It's also about the work that people do, the jobs we've held, labor and money, the flow of capital, how personal experience bumps up against the impersonal forces of capitalism.

I have always loved the tradition of the work song, which times poetry to the physical action of the body. It may actually challenge the nature of work by changing our mindset as we do it. The rhythm of the words restructures time. It induces a kind of ritualistic hypnosis, a rhythmic ecstasy. I also care about the hidden or underground tradition of the written poem about work, which stems from Hesiod's *Works and Days*. The ancient Greeks believed that poetry could also teach us how to keep bees and handle a plough.

I'm an urban poet and I've tried to think about the workplaces where my two fathers spent their lives hustling for a dollar. The language of those places also seems resonant for poetry. Hence the metaphors of "Cold Calls," the rotating sign that I saw for the company "Liberty Brass," my memory of one of my first jobs, filling orders on a second-story warehouse and reading Pablo Neruda. I read the Business Section of the *New York Times* for years and began to notate some of the terms that had entered our lexicon, such as "Mergers and Acquisitions." Wordsworth helped trigger my thinking when he observed, "Getting and spending, we lay waste our powers." And he wrote that when the nineteenth century was just getting started.

Yusef Komunyakaa

Yusef Komunyakaa's *Neon Vernacular: New and Selected Poems*
(Wesleyan University Press, 1994) won the Kingsley Tufts Poetry Award
and the Pulitzer Prize. His most recent collections of poetry include
Testimony: A Tribute to Charlie Parker (Wesleyan University Press, 2013)
and *Emperor of Water Clocks* (Farrar, Straus and Giroux, 2015). He served
as a chancellor of the Academy of American Poets from 1999 to 2005.
Currently he serves as Distinguished Senior Poet in New York
University's graduate creative writing program.

༄ A Prayer for Workers

Bless the woman, man, & child
   who honor Earth by opening shine
in the soil—the splayed hour
   between dampness & dust—to plant
a few seedlings in furrows, & then pray
   for cooling rain. Bless the fields,
the catch, the hunt, & the wild fruit,
   & let no one go hungry tonight
or tomorrow. Let the wind & birds
   seed a future ferried into villages
& towns the other side of mountains
   along nameless rivers. Bless those
born with hands made to do work,
   hewn timbers & stone raised from earth
& shaped in circles, who know the geometry
   of corners, & please level the foundation
& pitch a roof so good work isn't diminished
   by rain. Bless the farmer with clouds
in his head, who lugs baskets of dung
   so termites can carve their hives
that hold water long after a downpour
   has gone across the desert & seeds
sprout into a contiguous greening.
   Bless the iridescent beetle working
to haul the heavens down, to journey
   from moon dust to excrement.
The wage-slave's two steps from Dickens's
   tenements among a den of thieves,
blind soothsayers who know shambles
   where migrants feathered the nests
of straw bosses as the stonecutters
   perfect profiles of robber barons
in granite & marble in town squares
   along highways paved for Hollywood.
Bless souls laboring in sweatshops,
   & each calabash dipper of water,

the major & minor litanies & ganglia
    dangling from promises at the mouth
of the cave, the catcher of vipers at dawn
    in the canebrake & flowering fields,
not for the love of money but for bread
    & clabber on a thick gray slab table,
for the simple blessings in a small town
    of the storytellers drunk on grog.
Bless the cobbler, molding leather
    on his oaken lasts, kneading softness
& give into a red shoe & a work boot,
    never giving more to one than the other,
& also the weaver with closed eyes,
    whose fingers play the loops & ties,
as if nothing else matters, daybreak
    to sunset, as stories of a people
grow into an epic stitched down
    through the ages, the outsider artists,
going from twine & hue, cut & tag,
    an ironmonger's credo of steam rising
from buckets & metal dust, & the clang
    of a hammer against an anvil,
& the ragtag ones, the motley crew
    at the end of the line, singing ballads
& keeping time on a battered tin drum.

ᔍ Cape Coast Castle

I made love to you, & it loomed there.
We sat on the small veranda of the cottage,
& listened hours to the sea talk.
I didn't have to look up to see if it was still there.
For days, it followed us along polluted beaches
where the boys herded cows
& the girls danced for the boys,
to the moneychanger,
& then to the marketplace.

It went away when the ghost of my mother
found me sitting beneath a palm,
but it was in the van with us on a road trip to the country
as we zoomed past thatch houses.
It was definitely there when a few dollars
exchanged hands & we were hurried
through customs, past the guards.
I was standing in the airport in Amsterdam,
sipping a glass of red wine, half lost in Van Gogh's
swarm of colors, & it was there, brooding in a corner.
I walked into the public toilet, thinking of W.E.B.
buried in a mausoleum, & all his books & papers
going to dust, & there it was, in that private moment,
the same image: obscene because it was built
to endure time, stronger than their houses & altars.
The seeds of melon. The seeds of okra in trade winds
headed to a new world. I walked back into the throng
of strangers, but it followed me. I could see the path
slaves traveled, & I knew when they first saw it
all their high gods knelt on the ground.
Why did I taste salt water in my mouth?
We stood in line for another plane,
& when the plane rose over the city
I knew it was there, crossing the Atlantic.
Not a feeling, but a longing. I was in Accra
again, gazing up at the vaulted cathedral ceiling
of the compound. I could see the ships at dusk
rising out of the lull of "Amazing Grace," cresting
the waves. The governor stood on his balcony,
holding a sword, pointing to a woman
in the courtyard, saying, That one.
Bring me that tall, ample wench.
Enslaved hands dragged her to the center,
then they threw buckets of water on her,
but she tried to fight. They penned her to the ground.
She was crying. They prodded her up the stairs. One step,
& then another. Oh, yeah, she still had some fight in her,
but the governor's power was absolute. He said,

There's a tyranny of language in my fluted bones.
There's a poetry on every page of the good book.
There's God's work to be done in a forsaken land.
There's a whole tribe in this one, but I'll break them
before they're in the womb, before they're conceived,
before they're even thought of. Come, up here,
don't be afraid, up here to the governor's quarters,
up here where laws are made. I haven't delivered
the head of Pompey or John the Baptist
on a big silver tray, but I own your past,
present, & future. You're special.
You're not like the others. Yes,
I'll break you with fists & cat-o'-nine.
I'll thoroughly break you, head to feet,
but sister I'll break you most
dearly with sweet words.

From the Poet

When I think of capital and contemporary society, I inevitably trek back into biblical history. I have always been troubled by the ultimate downfall of the Christ figure, who suffered a lynching after he thrashed the money lenders from the temple. Today's system of money lending bears another kind of oppressive brutality—one designed to pit groups of poor people against one another. I don't dare go one hundred feet in front of the White House without thinking about the free labor exploited to build it, especially now, in relation to today's populist theatrical illusions of grandeur that seem to have infiltrated the hearts and minds of the have-nots.

In his 1968 Poor People's Campaign, a multiethnic, interfaith coalition, Dr. Martin Luther King embraced the power of protest for civil rights and for equity for all of the poor—white and black. He knew he was confronting the cornerstone of institutional racism and oppression, and he knew he was in grave danger. History repeats, and again the martyr is nailed to the dogwood, or spotted in the crosshairs.

Poetry is one way to respond to the idolatry of money and the oppressive injustice of usury. Poetry can create an atmosphere of reflection but also one of action because it asks the reader to reflect with the poet and to observe what may otherwise seem invisible.

Mary Jo Bang

Mary Jo Bang is the author of eight books of poems, including
A Doll for Throwing (Graywolf, 2017) and *Elegy* (Graywolf, 2007), which
received the National Book Critics Circle Award. She has published a
translation of Dante's *Inferno* (Graywolf, 2012) and her translation
of *Purgatorio* is forthcoming (Graywolf, 2021). A recipient of the
Guggenheim fellowship, a Hodder fellowship from Princeton, and a
fellowship from the American Academy in Berlin, she teaches
creative writing at Washington University in St. Louis.

∾ A Woman Overheard Speaking

A woman overheard speaking to the machine: Going backwards today to
when I first heard fate saying how poor I would be, What can badness
bring you, I wanted to ask. Under that surface, a seam indicating time is
worth nothing much. Sitting here, my brain melts in at the edge, a clock
wrapped in cloth. The idle machine is a crowd encased in ice. The factory
buzzes at four, followed by the jolt of an alarm at the perimeter. Green
leopards enter, barely visible against the gray-green background. I call
them my dollar bills. I keep my fingers crossed and cut to the quick. I was
first in pieces, now I'm fewer and further between. I shop for answers to
inane questions. Yes, I left early. Yes, I worked for a while. Yes, the weight
of exhaustion sent me to bed. Yes, I've been told I'm a test case. An
example of what not to do with what I don't know. A slight oscillation
while *on* switches into action, then the bimodal fevered bland. I hold onto
what little motion there is. It keeps me from toppling into the through
hole. Habit flattens the stairwell, a floor rises up to meet face and feet,
forming a level plane. An incessant needle mimes in and out. For me it's
like fucking air.

∾ Wall Street

The trapeze artist above
                    is invested in space.
She attends to the arc the bar makes
                    the way you'd watch a movie
where a star who looks like you swings on a swing.

It's true you know how to wait
                    although I don't know that
that counts as knowledge.

I heard a banker say to Monsignor this morning,
                    I'm certain God wishes me well.

A rat's face at the window next to me
is stone and the wind isn't blowing.
A rat's face sometimes reminds me
of what one sees in a morning mirror:

nose, eyes, a head, some hair.
Five racehorses, neck to neck,
each with four feet off the ground:
yet another classic example
of time seeming to be standing still.
Everyone with money knows that
flying from Pisa to France is a pain
since you have to change plans in Brussels.
As I said to Monsignor this morning,
I'm certain God wishes me well.

From the Poet

It feels rude to write about how terrifying and deadening machine work is while I sit at a computer. To write backwards to an earlier memory of having nothing and going nowhere. Of growing up and into the inheritance-narrative of marrying and becoming a mothering workforce of one, feeding fabric to an eager needle, clickety-clickety-click. Here is a curtain. Here is a shirt. Here is a child. I made it. A man would come in at the end of the day and ask for food to be served at a table. Nothing looked good to me. Is it only a question of class at the crossroads of history? Has it all changed, or has nothing changed? I know what I did but that doesn't address the issue of what can be done. I learned to type. I became a secretary. I worked one day in a garment factory. I kept looking at the clock. The basket kept filling with what had no worth aside from the pennies I'd be paid if ever I learned to sew straight. A life is a small thing except to the one living it. I'm talking about money.

Minnie Bruce Pratt

Minnie Bruce Pratt's second book of poetry, *Crime Against Nature*,
on being a lesbian mother, received the James Laughlin Award from
the Academy of America Poets in 1989 and was reissued by
A Midsummer Night's Press in 2013. Her tenth book, *Inside the
Money Machine* (Carolina Wren Press, 2011), has been described as
"stunning anti-capitalist poetics in action." Her new book *Magnified*
is forthcoming from Wesleyan University Press. She is a managing
editor of *Workers World/Mundo Obrero* newspaper.

∾ Looking for Work

I don't have a job yet, all right? You ask every time you call.
Jobs don't grow on trees. The way my pa walked through
Los Angeles, past palms crowned with rats' nests, on foot
in the land of cars. He'd been a chauffeur to the stars,
a coalminer, he'd made tires, he'd worked in every state but
two, and he could not find a job. The thigh piston lifts the knee,
drives the foot down into the ground. *How can this be?*
I say, fast breath, as I drop my application into the slot.

What did he like about work under ground? Was it the dark
or was it the breaking through? The dark line of connection,
the seam of ore, a sentence to be read by other miners and him.
It ran for miles, it never ends until the money men sit down
to squeeze the world in their hands. They can afford to wait
until diamonds are done. Meanwhile, we struggle in the sun,
like people lined up by the church, dressed go-to-meeting neat.
When I ask *Why? Food,* says one man, turning away. Yes, I'm afraid
that will be me. They said they'd hire me back the next day,
at my pay ten years ago. But I still have some savings, and my pride.

∾ Picketing the Bargain Store

They say: *We do not lack imagination.* They watch
the boss try to harness them with word, threat, and trick.
They know he is out front getting photographed under
the red-white-and-blue Grand Opening banner, there
to remind shoppers of a national holiday, a victor's war.
They know they are inside fourteen hours a day, seven
days a week, once three days straight, no break,
one pizza a day to eat. Inside, they bend, grasp, lift
up onto the shelves the stuff for someone else's house,
bottles of bleach, welcome mats, thin pastel towels,
the green-and-gold peacock porcelain clocks,
each crowned head arched back to look at how well
it carries time in its belly. They make $2.74 an hour,
no benefits, no overtime. At night they sleep on the floor

of someone else's 99 Cent Dream Bargain Store.
They are here today to say: *¡Basta! Not us, not any more.*

Five workers say: *Enough.* Not enough yet for the police to lift
the blue barricades off the truck and set them to guard the store.

∾ Playing the Guitar Underground

The man with the guitar sings *mi pobre corazón,*
his heart and an empty hat at his feet as he sings
on the island between the local and the express train.
On the way north, past the muscled mudflat river,
there was some shelter on the border that's not a border.
The bridge by the rattling cottonwoods, or a boxcar
near the *barelas* in Albuquerque, like the one where
he was born, one of eleven, five did not survive.
El perdito niño, his infant's white gown pinned
with tiny *milagros,* the bent leg, the pierced heart,
the double eyes that see forward and backward,
the house, the helping hand, the note that says,
Living on the street for so long and I am tired
and always hungry and sick, please help. A picture,
the three of them, *Venimos desde muy lejos.* Boxcars
head due east between watermelon-red and apple-red
mountains, New Mexico-South Carolina. But when
he comes to the green valley there is only one apple
after another in his hand, bleeding heart of Jesus,
take it and eat. Like the red rose he holds, standing
all day at the entrance to the highway tunnel under-
ground. He'll trade his red for your silver, what's left
of the twists of fish and snakes and quetzal-tailed birds,
the silver that flew away from there to here over the Gulf,
or what's left of wages sent north from the *maquiladoras.*
He says that's NAFTA, *el tratado de libre comercio,*
that's how anyone without someone in the U.S. starves
or leaves the village to follow money that's free to move.

In the broad-brimmed bowl of the hat, coins pile up
like grain, something to send home to replace the corn
that no one can afford to grow now in Michoacán.

∼ The Dow Turns Red

At the mini-mart: *"Major Bank Fails in the South."*
Wall Street quivers. This street not so far north.
Some three or four Black men under a sycamore
or seated in the sun, talking each other through.
The lopsided houses, the cracked glass windows
waiting to swallow the last narrow icing of cold.
The jobs went south, further south, Wall Street
moving money around the world for profit, the sun
never sets on capital gain. What does that mean?
People somewhere else paid less to work more,
one day they're out of work under noon's glare, or
another man I pass, doing car repairs on the street:
Trying to make a living. What can I say? *Me too.*
I'm wondering how long my job will last, a place
to go every day, a shade, a shape we live inside
even as giant invisible hands hold and squeeze,
even as they fail and fall open. The Dow turns red
in the wreck, but the color of our blood isn't money.

From the Poet

For three months in the spring of 2002, when I was out of work as a teacher, Milt Neidenberg taught me Marxist economics. Milt was an eighty-year-old former steelworker, union organizer, and communist.

Milt also loved Shakespeare. He had briefly been a college English major when he got out of the Navy after WWII. Five years before we started discussing Marxism, we were already talking about poetry. I would ask him: "How does an artist/writer participate in 'the revolutionary process'? How does a poet 'expose the ruling class'?"

And then I lost my job and had time to study with Milt. Every week I would come with questions about Marxist economics. "A McDonald's worker cooks a hamburger that gets eaten. Not like a car! Where's the surplus value?"

Milt said: "The challenge in organizing under high-tech is this experiential gap. The McDonald's hamburger cooked and bagged by a worker is given to a customer who eats it immediately, and the product of the workers' labor has vanished, seemingly. The current socialization of labor is . . . marked by subdivision of tasks into smaller and smaller units of production, and into more and more geographically distant or isolated units of production. The challenge is to make visible the hidden creation of value."

And then Milt said: "The enslavement of people was visible in a way that wage slavery is not, because the exploitation of workers through wage slavery is hidden in the abstraction of exchange value, i.e. money."

I asked him: "Is it possible for poetry to make this hidden process visible, felt, and thus known by a reader? Can poetry aid in bringing self-consciousness to us as workers in this process?"

Milt: "Difficult!"

My first "homework assignment" from him was to make visible that value in a flier for the Stop Workfare campaign. People on public assistance, the majority women of color, were being forced to do city maintenance jobs for no pay in New York City.

Milt never gave me an assignment to write poems to make visible our value as workers and the connections between us. I had attempted to write a few such poems earlier, when I read *The Communist Manifesto* for the first time. I had discovered to my astonishment how beautiful the language of Marx and Engels is. I'd said to myself, "If the economists can write such poetry, what would happen if a poet tried to write their Marxist economics?"

The poems of my book *Inside the Money Machine* are the result.

Because when Milt said to me: "First theory, then applied theory," he meant poetry, too.

George Perreault

George Perreault's most recent collection, *Bodark County*
(Grayson Books, 2016), features poems in the voices of characters
living on the Llano Estacado. He has received awards from the Nevada
Arts Council and the Washington Poets Association, and has served
as a visiting writer in New Mexico, Montana, and Utah.

∽ Buster McKinney: Economics

We was grabbin a bite, no cloth-napkin fancy place,
just some big chain, eat up, throw your own stuff away,
most folks pitchin in and moving on, not thinkin twice
same's we pump our own gas everwhere except maybe
Oregon, and I was rememberin my granddaddy one time
I was clearin off a table, he says, don't be doin that,
that's somebody's job, and I guess perhaps I looked
at him kinda sideways, like he was being mister high
and mighty, like he was too good maybe bus a table.
But he was an oldtimer, you know, one of them
Depression guys, branded by those hard times,
so he explained it to me, real slow, just making sure—

It's not *somebody else's* job, not like too many folks
nowadays, let the next guy pick up the slack—but that's
somebody's job, not a good one, not one you'd care to
stand in line for if you needn't, but there's plenty
fellers have to take whatever they can, when and where,
like us back from the elevator droppin our milo, guys
paid for sweeping the floors, then the operators and
supervisors and up the line, commodities brokers
and the like—got nothing against anyone tryin to scratch
out a living, and I'll be damned I take a man's job away.

Well, I guess that kinda stuck somehow, then come to me
fillin up the truck, checkin my oil and catchin my
reflection in an ADM cap, sumbitches that fixed feed prices
while back, so I look round and I got a Morales hat, that
feedlot down Devine, got Komatsu, New Holland—jeezus,
just a walkin billboard like them kids payin good money to
advertise Nike or Adidas while the rich go label-free, buy
everthing they want, send kids off to die, them what never
served a day, or come back denied medical or anything else,
us settlin for any job people not tryin to kill you outright.

∾ James Hardesty: Burrito

Was this homeless guy standin outside Taco Bell
tryin to stay dry in this welcome rain—well, for us
anyways, raising thirty crops up on the caprock—
so on the way out I handed him an extra burrito I got,
figurin it might be today's best meal and hot besides.

Kynzie she asked about that and I said for your granddad,
so I had to tell her bout when he mustered out from 'Nam,
wasn't no real hurry getting home, hung in LA some time,
getting work here and there, just feelin out the world, and
one of the jobs was a cafeteria downtown, edge of things.

He took orders, which he was used to doin, though these felt
more like requests, on the graveyard shift, which everyone
in 'Nam was used to doing, more ways than one, and there was
this woman come in regular, real old, just so frail everyway
you might think of, penciled eyebrows, thin thin hair,

always wearing the same faded red coat, black hat, would
ask a cup of hot water, then use the ketchup packs to make
a kinda tomato soup, eat the crackers from the table, never
order anything, go back out into the night—maybe she had
three four places on her rounds so they'd get her twice a week.

The cook, your granddad said, he would get all upset, say
throw her out, but wouldn't, and the cook maybe he didn't
dare, so she kept comin back and was part of the night crowd,
would come in when the clubs closed down, the comics and the
bartenders and all, talkin over their troubles, maybe tryin

different routines for each other—no, if you do the Duke, you
gotta get that walk, all pigeon-toes, important as the drawl—
demonstratin in the spaces between tables, same people
every night, and to your granddad she was part of that, and it got
so he'd whisper a couple of them, make a mistake on the order

then he'd tell the cook it was a screw-up, they had an extra
grilled cheese, and he'd slide it on this lady's table, ask if maybe
she could help out please so he wouldn't get in trouble with that

cook, and she'd nod and not say nothin, eat that sandwich as a
favor to this kid, being such a nice lady and all.

So it's a buck and change, I told Kynzie, not so much for us,
but I look him in the eyes, ask could he help with this wrong order
else I'll give it to the hounds and they'll get all squirty-pants.
Way I figure, it's what your granddad would do, extra buck
on the Sunday plate, it don't mean that much.

From the Poet

My parents' families were farmers and carpenters during the Depression,
typical Americans immersed in a culture which even then attempted to
commodify everything and surrendered so much in the process. As they
hoped and prayed, their children did well, even prospered. We have houses
and cars and health care; we swim somewhere between the heedlessly rich
and the desperately poor, inoculated against the worst effects of capitalism—
or so it seemed before the coming of COVID-19. But even before this latest
financial calamity, I have experienced moments of rage and of shame—
what we do as a country, how little I have done to help. Some of these
moments have turned into stories, some into poems.

Poetry may be better when it deals with the moment, rather than the
grand sweep of things—less about the daily traffic surge into our great cit-
ies and more about those first seconds after the car has spun uncontrollably
across traffic, leaving you to sit in the shuddering quiet, breathing. Poetry—
mine at least—is not about monetary policy or the effects of micro-loans
in developing countries or the obscene inequity that corrupts everything
it touches. Poetry is the phone echoing in a bare room, an old woman's
eyes sparking with recognition, the crisp smell of a new baseball glove.

I seek to write about the life that connects us all, about true wealth. As
evidenced in these poems, I use the voices of "fly-over Americans" whose
views are much more nuanced and thoughtful than commonly assumed.
In many ways, the heartland of this country is tribal enough to intuit that
pursuit of individual wealth can only come at the expense of the rest of the
village, and that these days we're all citizens of the same tribe.

Sharon Olds

Sharon Olds has received many awards for her work, including the
inaugural San Francisco Poetry Center Award, the National Book Critics
Circle Award, and, for her 2012 collection, *Stag's Leap* (Knopf), the Pulitzer
and T.S. Eliot Prizes. Her recent collections include *Arias* (Knopf, 2019)
and *Odes* (Knopf, 2016). She currently teaches in the graduate
creative writing program at New York University.

∾ Left-Wife Bop

Suddenly I remember the small bar
of gold my young husband bought
and buried near our old farmhouse. During our
divorce—as much ours as any
Sunday dinner was, or what was
called the nap which followed it—
he wanted to go to the house, one last
time. *Please, not with her,*
please, and he said *All right*, and I don't know
why, when I figured it out, later,
that he'd gone to dig up our bar of gold,
I didn't mind. I think the reason is how
even it was, between us, how even
we divided the chores, even though he was
the wage-earner, how evenly
the bounty of pleasure fell between us—
wait, what's a bounty? Like a kidnap fee?
He fell in love with her because I
didn't suit him any more—
nor him, me, though I could not see it, but he
saw it for me. Even, even,
our playing field—we inspired in each other
a generousness. And he did not give
his heart to his patients, but I gave my secrets
to you, dear strangers, and his, too—
unlike the warbling of coming, I sang
for two. Uneven, uneven, our scales
of contentment went slowly askew, and when he
hopped off, on the ground floor, and I
sailed through the air, poetic justice
was done. So when I think of him
going with his pick and shovel to exactly where he
knew the ingot was, and working his
way down, until the air
touched it and released its light,
I think he was doing what I'd been doing, but I'd

got a little ahead of him—he was
redressing the balance, he was leading his own life.

∽ Money

Filthy lucre, dough, lettuce,
jack, folderola, wherewithal, the ready,
simoleons, fins, tenners, I savored
the smell of money, sour, like ink,
and salty-dirty, like strangers' thumbs,
we touch it like our mutual skin
tattooed with webs—orb and ray—and with
Abe, and laurel leaves, and Doric
pillars, and urns, acanthus, mint scales,
a key. I liked the feel of it,
like old, flannel pajamas, the fiber
worn to a gloss, and the 2 × 6
classic size, which does not change
from generation unto generation as the
hand grows to encompass it—
and I liked the numerals, the curly
5, and the 1 the grandmother president
seems to be guarding,
as if the government would protect your identity
if they could find it, and they didn't have to kill
too many of your relatives
to get at it. Poor identity,
glad-handed so long, the triangle head all
eye, over the pyramid torso,
parent over child, rock over scissors,
ANNUIT COEPTIS over NOVUS
ORDO SECLORUM. A dime a week
if you did your jobs and did not act morally
horrible, which meant, for some, a dime
a year. Now if my mom had paid me, to hit me,
I could have had a payola account,
and been a child whore magnate. No question

what it meant, to see the interest mount up,
the wad of indenture, legal tender—
no question to me what a bill was,
its cry sounded like the diesel train's
green cry, it was a ticket to ride.

From the Poet

"Money" was written in 1999 or 2000. Maybe I had looked closely at a
dollar bill for the first time, like Muriel Rukeyser at a cockroach, in her
poem "Saint Roach." I'm sure I felt happy when, after writing it, I thought
that not many poems had dedicated themselves to describing money—the
outward and visible sign of it. Reading it again, now, I like the thumbs,
skin, pajamas, and grandmother in it—and I'm glad inequality of power in
societies and families came into it, as well, along with some Latin, and a
reference to violence toward children. Talk about agency!—"child whore
magnate." (Occupy! Resist!) And then the word *tender*, and the color *green*,
and the desire to become a wage-earner, in order to move out and move on.
Parents and governments are seen as dangerous, and capitalism is treated
with hungry if not greedy childish relish.

The Bop was typed first in 2008. (Like all my poems, it was initially writ-
ten by hand in ballpoint in a lined, grocery-store notebook. I write a lot of
poems, and only a fraction of them get typed or sent out or put in a book.)
Once again, I bet I was happy a "non-poetic" subject had occurred to me.
I'm glad to have written a poem about a bar of gold—like a fairy-tale image.
I'm glad also about the nap, the kidnap, the "Please, not with her," the war-
bling, the seesaw, and my sense of the truthfulness of the poem, the equal-
ity, the fairness. It isn't really a Bop, of course—the form created by Afaa
Michael Weaver one summer at Cave Canem—but I felt my poem had
learned from the sense of poetic argument of a Bop, and I wanted to pay its
inventor homage. (September, 2018)

Wendy Barker

Wendy Barker's most recent collections include *Gloss*
(Saint Julian Press, 2020), *One Blackbird at a Time* (BkMk Press, 2015),
winner of the John Ciardi Prize, and the chapbook *Shimmer* (Glass Lyre
Press, 2019). With Dave Parsons, she coedited *Far Out: Poems of the 60s*
(Wings Press, 2016). Recipient of NEA and Rockefeller fellowships,
she teaches at the University of Texas at San Antonio.

∽ Planishing

The steel head of a hammer pounded on the surface of a newly shaped bowl, platter, or spoon. Panel-beating hammers, slappers, and neck hammers. Finishing, smoothing, the last step.

Silver underground is mottled, pitted, rough or ropy, charcoal gray or sooty black. The miners drill holes, shove in sticks of dynamite, blast the rock wall. They pulverize the chunks they haul to the earth's surface and pour the powder into vats of water mixed with acid to separate the silver from copper or lead, baser metals.

Heat in those mines will reach 120, humidity 100%. Dust-clogged air. Miners can lose their hearing from the blasts, be torn to shreds by premature explosions, or roasted alive in underground fires.

Pure silver is nearly white, lustrous, soft, ductile, malleable, coiled like snakes, like our intestines. Ideally, planished silver should be smooth as a pond's surface without a breeze. Or a mirror, so glossy we see our faces.

∽ Tombstone, 1962

Just married when I lived there. In a trailer—single-wide, 8′ × 48′ — with the wedding silver. Ten place settings, knives, butter knives, dinner forks, salad forks, dessert, soup spoons. Reed & Barton's "The Lark." All neatly lined up and enclosed in a zippered tarnish-proof case. Not enough money from the paycheck to buy milk. Beer, potato chips, but not milk. I needed more calcium, leg cramps in the night. I'd get up, stomp on that foot, stretch my calf muscle, turn on the light. Open the kitchen cabinet, unzip the cloth case. Fondle those pieces, their cool weight, the liquid-silky spoons, graceful curves of the knives' handles. Which, I knew even then, were hollow.

∽ On Silver Spoons

The Golliwog spoon, we called it, the handle shaped like a head with heavy-lidded eyes and a thick-lipped mouth. Coddled eggs, Cream of Wheat in that spoon. And someone gave me a Golliwog doll—kinky black hair, clown-red mouth. A second silver spoon: simple, ridged lines leading from the handle to the shallow bowl. "Tiffany & Co.," "Sterling" stamped on the back.

Two baby cups: one upright, sterling, from Tiffany's, straight-sided, no decorations. The other: urn-shaped, graceful, flowers twining around the handle, leaves spiraling the circumference. Orange juice, chocolate milk from both.

Bridge club friends of my New Jersey grandparents gave me the plain spoon and cup. But the others came from Tony, my father's devil-may-care best friend who'd waltz double forte down Broadway, bouncing my cautious father out of his Presbyterian gloom. Both were besotted with my mother, but dependable Daddy won out, while Tony joined the diplomatic corps, moved to Bogotá. Colombia: a country I'd never heard of till years after that silver had been packed away.

No sterling stamp on the flowery cup or the Golliwog spoon. Golliwog. A caricature of a caricature. My mother and father read me the books. "A horrid sight, the blackest gnome," ran Bertha Upton's prose. Entranced by the stories, Debussy composed "Golliwog's Cakewalk," but by the sixties I knew those characters were downright offensive, and cheered when librarians withdrew the books from their shelves.

I never met Tony. Not worth squat if it's not stamped sterling, says the jeweler. When was it I unpacked the Golliwog spoon? And realized it was probably an image of a god, maybe a Dolmen from Pre-Incan times. Or the San Agustin jaguar god—square nose, slanted eyes.

Two spoons, two cups, gifts for my birthing. Better than the spoon-like forceps that dented my scalp as I struggled into air. Forceps, a pair of spoons that molded me. Spoons: the Spanish, Greeks, Russians, Turks, and even Americans make music with them, like silvery castanets. The clink of two metals against each other. It took a long time for my head to reshape itself.

ᵔ Cleaning Silver

It's the indentations, places of repoussé, chasing, that remain blackened. The effects that took so long to create—the annealing, the work with steel punches, the chasing hammers. After giving up on the polish-soaked rag and digging in with a toothbrush, it's as if you're scrubbing more than tarnish, hunting for a story you haven't been told.

From the Poet

I didn't grow up with much silver, other than the forks, spoons, and knives that had been gifts for my parents' wedding in 1939. My childhood was spent in a series of cramped tract houses in working-class neighborhoods, in a family where money was always in short supply. However, my grandparents lived lavishly—my father's parents in suburban New Jersey and my mother's parents in England. The disconnect between the circumstances of my life as a girl and those of my grandparents never made sense, and around 2012 I began writing poems exploring that subject, often focusing on silver pieces I had inherited after my grandparents and then my parents died.

As a toddler, I possessed four pieces of silver that were my very own, gifts at my birth. I talk about these in "On Silver Spoons," musing on the significance and backgrounds of these little items. And I became increasingly fascinated with the dangerous processes involved with silver mining as well as the procedures for making silver pieces, as I explore in "Planishing." I also began writing about the strange value silver possesses—so that a young married couple with little money, like my former husband and me in 1962, had a set of sterling place settings but barely enough funds for grocery shopping. Ultimately, silver became a controlling metaphor for a whole new manuscript of poems, my recently published book *Gloss*.

Robert Pinsky

Robert Pinsky's most recent book of poems is *At the Foundling Hospital* (Farrar, Straus and Giroux, 2016). His *Selected Poems* appeared in 2011, and his best-selling translation *The Inferno of Dante* in 1995, both from Farrar, Straus and Giroux. Videos from his "Art of Poetry" are at www.bu.edu/ artofpoetry/. He teaches in the MFA program at Boston University.

∾ Shirt

The back, the yoke, the yardage. Lapped seams,
The nearly invisible stitches along the collar
Turned in a sweatshop by Koreans or Malaysians

Gossiping over tea and noodles on their break
Or talking money or politics while one fitted
This armpiece with its overseam to the band

Of cuff I button at my wrist. The presser, the cutter,
The wringer, the mangle. The needle, the union,
The treadle, the bobbin. The code. The infamous blaze

At the Triangle Factory in nineteen-eleven.
One hundred and forty-six died in the flames
On the ninth floor, no hydrants, no fire escapes—

The witness in a building across the street
Who watched how a young man helped a girl to step
Up to the windowsill, then held her out

Away from the masonry wall and let her drop.
And then another. As if he were helping them up
To enter a streetcar, and not eternity.

A third before he dropped her put her arms
Around his neck and kissed him. Then he held
Her into space, and dropped her. Almost at once

He stepped to the sill himself, his jacket flared
And fluttered up from his shirt as he came down,
Air filling up the legs of his gray trousers—

Like Hart Crane's Bedlamite, "shrill shirt ballooning."
Wonderful how the pattern matches perfectly
Across the placket and over the twin bar-tacked

Corners of both pockets, like a strict rhyme
Or a major chord. Prints, plaids, checks,
Houndstooth, Tattersall, Madras. The clan tartans

Invented by mill-owners inspired by the hoax of Ossian,
To control their savage Scottish workers, tamed
By a fabricated heraldry: MacGregor,

Bailey, MacMartin. The kilt, devised for workers
To wear among the dusty clattering looms.
Weavers, carders, spinners. The loader,

The docker, the navvy. The planter, the picker, the sorter
Sweating at her machine in a litter of cotton
As slaves in calico headrags sweated in fields:

George Herbert, your descendant is a Black
Lady in South Carolina, her name is Irma
And she inspected my shirt. Its color and fit

And feel and its clean smell have satisfied
Both her and me. We have culled its cost and quality
Down to the buttons of simulated bone,

The buttonholes, the sizing, the facing, the characters
Printed in black on neckband and tail. The shape,
The label, the labor, the color, the shade. The shirt.

⌒ The Refinery

"... our language, forged in the dark by centuries of violent pressure,
underground, out of the stuff of dead life."

Thirsty and languorous after their long sleep
The old gods crooned: *Dry, dry.*
By railroad they set out across
The desert of stars to drink the world
Our mouths had soaked in sentences: a pollen-tinted
Slurry of passion and lapsed intention. The imagined
Taste made the savage deities hiss and snort.

Their long train clicked and sighed through
Gulfs of night between the planets, then down
Through pinewoods in the evening fog.
Fiery warehouse windows along a wharf.

Then dusk, a gash of neon: *Bar.*
Sluggish surf among the rocks, a moan
Of dreamy forgotten divinity fading
Against the walls of a town. Inside the train
A flash of dragonfly wings, an antlered brow,
Reptile stenches of immortal bodies.

Black night again, and then
After the bridge, a palace on the water:

The great Refinery—a million bulbs tracing
Its turreted boulevards. The castle of a person
Pronounced alive, the Corporation: a fictional
Lord real in law.

Barbicans and torches along the tracks
At the central tanks, the steel
Towers valved and chandeliered.

The muttering gods
Greedily penetrate those pavilions—
Libation of Benzine, Naphthalene, Asphalt,
Gasoline, Tar: syllables
Fractioned and cracked from unarticulated

Crude, the smeared remnant of life that fed
On itself in pitchy darkness when the gods
Were new—inedible, volatile
And sublimated afresh to sting
Our tongues who use it, refined from oil of stone.

The gods batten on the vats, and drink up
Lovecries and memorized Chaucer, lines from movies
Songs hoarded in memory: exiles' charms,
Sweet distillates of breath
Brewed and spent—as though
We were their aphids, or their bees,
That monstered up sweetness
For them while they dozed.

From the Poet

The most memorably beautiful sight of all my years in California was the immense Exxon refinery in Richmond. At night, covered in bulbs, an enchanted palace, visible on a return trip back to Berkeley from Yosemite. This palazzo of light above the water has poisoned the water, the soil, and the people of Richmond. Civil and criminal penalties have been paid, but the large-sounding sums don't matter to the corporate lord, the person-by-law who rules that illuminated castle.

The car that delivered my family and me to the Sierras and back, my electric lights, my recorded music, the machine I use to write these words, my clothes, the fillings in my teeth—all of these and more are enabled by that fuel of power, creative and destructive.

The poem "Shirt" involves the same dense weaving of goods and wrongs, from a different perspective. To identify a few of the threads is a life's work.

Petroleum, oil-of-stone, resembles language, perhaps the English language in particular: formed and enriched by the pressures of torture, expropriation, enslavement, disease, and rape, by waves of conquerors. As the epigraph of "The Refinery" indicates, language, petroleum products—all of civilization's goods and wrongs—are the product of suffering, genius, cruelty, and generosity on a scale beyond any one life. And they impinge on every life.

"To identify the threads . . ." What gods would have endowed such a creature, such an arrangement? What might be in it for them?

Martha Collins

Martha Collins's tenth book of poetry, *Because What Else Could I Do* (University of Pittsburgh Press, 2019), won the William Carlos Williams Award. Other recent books are *Night Unto Night* (Milkweed Editions, 2018) and *Admit One: An American Scrapbook* (University of Pittsburgh Press, 2016). Collins has also published four volumes of co-translated Vietnamese poetry and won numerous awards for her work.

∼ Middle

Start in the middle. Stay
there, if you can: up and down
the scale, but always come back to C.

*

Lost in the woods, supposing yourself in the middle
of the woods, you might in fact be very close to the edge.

Where, for that matter, does the middle of the woods begin?

And what about the middle of the story?

*

476–1453: call the Middle
Ages for information.

40–60: the cool or warm
days of middle age.

*

The middle class is the backbone of
this country. The back is the middle
bone of this class. The middle is back
of this country, the country's back
of the class. This bone, this country:

if what you have is a pretty good bone
for your soup, if you can remember
having no soup, if you think *class*
and remember 7th grade, then you might
say *middle* and think *the top* and mean *me*.

*

The middle of
the middle
is the middle.

*

Getting there, he never thought
he'd arrive. He had *places*
to go, he said, *the sky's*
the limit, but come from a three-
room shack with a coal stove,
he needed a roof he couldn't reach
as much as the old linoleum
floor. *More*, he said and said
to his kids. *Stop. That's enough.*

*

In the beginning we're in the middle,
or think we are. We're only on
the edge on the other edge.

*

If you live in the middle of town you don't see the edges.
In the middle of the country you don't see the seas.

If you live in the middle class you miss the others.
If you look in the middle distance you miss the point.

If you find a middle ground you can maybe hold it.
But the middle of the road is a risky place.

*

Above was once our blue
cover, movie screen with lights

at night. Now we think we hold
it up. Weightless, it gets heavy,

while the small hand
of *under* tugs and tugs.

∾ White Money

white	money	much
money	most	money
white	money	means
money	free	money
white	money	mine

"Your paycheck when it's signed by a white man."
www.urbandictionary.com

slaves hoeing picking bailing
carrying loading trundling cotton

butchering hogs mining mowing
men women children families

It's right on the money, said
John W. Jones, the black artist

who made paintings of the slave
images featured on southern currency

that was printed until the Civil War
in Boston New York Philadelphia

including also the goddess of money
with slaves in cotton fields behind:

white cotton gold coins black
faces hands white money

"Let me see the color of your money."

in front of a store

whistled or spoke or

$4000 paid by *Look*

so we know they said

they beat him shot him

in Money, Mississippi

"We established White Money
to make life easier for business persons."
www.whitemoney.com

white	money	white
paper	white	my
white	papers	white

From the Poet

"Middle" appears in my fourth collection, *Some Things Words Can Do* (1998), a book in which I employed multiple meanings, uses, and homonyms of single words as a way of thinking about converging and conflicting concepts. A number of fourteen-line poems in the book explore words like "Times" and "Races," and a few like "Middle" extend the exploration via a kind of collaging. I began the poem by thinking about the amorphous nature of the term "middle," and my own (then) middle age makes a brief appearance; but the question of class soon became central. When I was a child, being middle class felt like what I would now call the norm. Writing this poem, and obliquely exploring the origins of my immediate family's middle class-ness, led me to think about some of the complexities and problems of class itself.

"White Money," also a kind of collage, appears in an even more focused book: *White Papers* (2012), a collection of untitled but numbered poems that explore the question of what it means—historically, socially, personally— to be "white" in a racial and still racist society. (In the book, "White Money" appears simply as "29.") The collection grew out of the book-length poem *Blue Front* (2006), which focuses on a lynching my father witnessed as a child in Cairo, Illinois, its victim (predictably) an African American man. My primary perspective when I began was wondering how the lynching would have affected my father, but increasingly I began to think about what the event had to do with me. When the term "white papers" came into my mind, I knew I had a way of exploring that question.

Some of the "papers" are personal, a number of them focusing on my own very white childhood in Iowa; others use historical research, often in combination with personal experience. Except for the opening and closing riffs on "money" (which are related to poems like "Middle"), "White Money" is based almost entirely on research. But it follows a rule I made, that I would write only about places where I'd lived—New England, the Midwest, the West. This poem appears to violate that rule; but when I discovered that some of the Southern currency discussed in the poem was printed in Boston, I knew that I was an indirect beneficiary of this most telling form of exchange. No economist could have made a stronger connection between money and slavery than these bills themselves do: people *were* money.

For Further Reading

The following anthologies are kin to *The Poetry of Capital*. This list is not meant to be exhaustive but rather a next step for those who wish to contextualize and broaden the conversation we have had here.

Beckman, Josh, and Matthew Zapruder, editors. *State of the Union: Fifty Political Poems*. Wave Books, 2008.

This short, nimble anthology includes one poem by each of fifty contemporary poets, surveying the political landscape of America circa 2008. Jazzy, passionate, and progressive in outlook, these poems explore a range of subjects including the death of Coretta Scott King and George W. Bush–era politics, especially the 2003 invasion of Iraq.

Coles, Nicholas, and Janet Zandy, editors. *American Working-Class Literature*. Oxford University Press, 2007.

This 900-plus-page anthology includes what its editors call "writing about America's working people"—a rich focus. Unique in its historically comprehensive approach, the compendium includes work from the mid-1600s all the way to the early 2000s.

Coles, Nicholas and Peter Oresick, editors. *For a Living: The Poetry of Work*. University of Illinois Press, 1995.

A companion volume to *Working Classics* (see below), this anthology focuses on non-industrial work—jobs classified as white collar, domestic, clerical, managerial, and technical. Most of the poems were written in the post-industrial 1980s and 1990s, providing useful background for the labor poems in *The Poetry of Capital*.

Cushway, Philip and Michael Warr, editors. *Of Poetry & Protest: From Emmett Till to Trayvon Martin.* W. W. Norton, 2016.

This large-format anthology collects the work of forty-three African American poets, mostly contemporary, exploring the struggle for racial justice. The anthology provides particularly useful historical context, including personal essays by the poets, political posters, and full-page photographs

Marsh, John, editor. *You Work Tomorrow: An Anthology of American Labor Poetry, 1929–41.* University of Michigan Press, 2007.

John Marsh unearths Depression-era poems that originally appeared in labor-union publications, sometimes anonymously or under pseudonym. Organized by union, this collection is notable as a historical record, as well as for the liveliness of the poems. With an introduction by poet Jim Daniels.

Oresick, Peter, and Nicholas Coles, editors. *Working Classics: Poems on Industrial Life.* University of Illinois Press, 1990.

This anthology contains poems about blue-collar workers, the men and women who ran the factories, mills, and refineries that bolstered America's post-WWII prosperity and who suffered through the deindustrialization of the 1970s and 1980s. Seventy-five poets are included, most from the baby-boom generation.

Acknowledgments

We would like to end with some thank-yous. First, to editor in chief Nathan MacBrien, managing editor Adam Mehring, art director Jennifer Conn, and especially to Press director Dennis Lloyd, whose faith in the vision of this anthology gave it a home. We are grateful to all who submitted to the open call and to the forty-four poets found in this volume, especially to the late Tony Hoagland and Jane Mead. We thank also Trinity College's Department of English, Trinity's Faculty Research Fund, the University of Hartford Faculty Senate, and Dean Katherine Black of the College of Arts and Sciences at the University of Hartford for funds and leave time to support our editing work. And a shout out to the folks behind the counters at Cosi and Hartford Baking Company in West Hartford. Finally, our endless gratitude to Joe, Fran, Riley, and Tiny, for the love and support that made this book possible.

We gratefully acknowledge the following organizations and individuals for permission to reprint copyrighted material.

Robert Avery, "The Leisure Class" from *New Madrid* and "Odds Are." Used by permission of the poet.

David Baker, "Postmodernism" and "Midwest Ode" from *Changeable Thunder*. Copyright © 2001 by David Baker. Reprinted with permission of The Permissions Company, Inc., on behalf of the University of Arkansas Press, www.uapress.com. Author photo by Katherine Baker.

Devon Balwit, "Minding the Gap" from *Rising Phoenix Review*, "Un-American" from *WineDrunk Sidewalk*, and "invocation." Used by permission of the poet.

Mary Jo Bang, "Wall Street" from *The Last Two Seconds*. Copyright © 2015 by Mary Jo Bang. Reprinted with permission of The Permissions

Company, Inc., on behalf of Graywolf Press, www.graywolfpress.org. "A Woman Overheard Speaking" used by permission of the poet. Author photo by Matt Valentine.

Wendy Barker, "Planishing," "Tombstone, 1962," "On Silver Spoons," and "Cleaning Silver" from *Gloss*. Copyright © 2020 by Wendy Barker. Reprinted with permission of Saint Julian Press, www.saintjulianpress.com.

John Bradley, "As Blood Is the Fruit of the Heart" from *Spontaneous Mummification*. Copyright © 2020 by John Bradley. Used by permission of SurVision Books. "What Money Can Buy" from *Fifth Wednesday Journal*. Used by permission of the poet. Author photo by Jana Brubaker.

Susan Briante, "Mother Is Marxist" from *The Market Wonders*. Copyright © 2016 by Susan Briante. Reprinted with permission of The Permissions Company, Inc., on behalf of Ahsahta Press, www.ahsahtapress.org. Author photo by Bear Guerra.

Xochiquetzal Candelaria, "Matter" from *Empire*. Copyright © 2011. Reprinted with permission of the University of Arizona Press. "Surrender #4: Take Notice, Take Nothing" from *Other Musics: New Latina Poetry*, edited by Cynthia Cruz (University of Oklahoma Press, 2019), and "Boom." Used by permission of the poet. Author photo by Gabriela Candelaria.

Alan Chazaro, "The Cowboy Shirts" from *Iron Horse Review* and "El Paletero's Song." Used by permission of the poet.

Martha Collins, "Middle" from *Some Things Words Can Do* (The Sheep Meadow Press, 1998). Used by permission of the poet. "White Money" from *White Papers*. Copyright © 2012 by Martha Collins. Reprinted with permission of the University of Pittsburgh Press. Author photo by Doug Macomber.

Will Cordeiro, "Piecework," "Smoke," and "Spambot." Used by permission of the poet.

Diana Marie Delgado, "Free Cheese and Butter," "Man of the House," and "La Puente" from *Tracing the Horse*. Copyright © 2019 by Diana Marie Delgado. Reprinted with permission of The Permissions Company, Inc., on behalf of BOA Editions, Ltd., boaeditions.org. Author photo by Felicia Zamora.

Mark Doty, "Air Rights" from *American Poetry Review*. Used by permission of the poet. Author photo by Rachel Eliza Griffiths.

Denise Duhamel, "$100,000," "$400,000," and "$600,000" from *Ka-Ching!* Copyright © 2009 by Denise Duhamel. Reprinted with permission of the University of Pittsburgh Press. Author photo by Amira Hadla.

Ross White, "Dark Money" from *Tin House* and "Savings & Loan" from *Barrow Street*. Used by permission of the poet. Author photo by Sophia Chizhikova.

Crystal Williams, "Detroit as Brewster Projects" and "At the Water" from *Detroit as Barn*. Copyright © 2014 by Crystal Williams. Reprinted with permission of Lost Horse Press. Author photo by the Fitzgerald Photo/Maine Headshot Studio.

Kathleen Winter, "Country Club Fourth of July" from *Barrow Street*, "The Grammar of Ornament" from *32 Poems*, and "Hipster Squid." Used by permission of the poet.

David Wojahn, "Ghost Mall: Richmond, Virginia" and "Piñata." Used by permission of the poet. Author photo by Noelle Watson.

B ENJAMIN S. G ROSSBERG is the director of creative writing
at the University of Hartford. His books include *Space Traveler* and
Sweet Core Orchard, winner of a Lambda Literary Award.
His latest collection is *My Husband Would.*

C LARE R OSSINI is the artist-in-residence in the
English Department at Trinity College, where she teaches creative
writing and directs an outreach program in a core-city public school.
Her books include *Lingo, Winter Morning with Crow*—winner of the
Akron Poetry Prize—and *Selections from the Claudia Poems.*